REFUGE

a collection of four plays

HOME \ PP Cranney
The YUM YUM ROOM \ Stephen House
CROWDED HOUSE \ John Romeril
The BRIDGE \ Chris Thompson

CURRENCY PRESS
The performing arts publisher

CURRENCY PLAYS

First published in 2009
by Currency Press Pty Ltd,
PO Box 2287, Strawberry Hills, NSW, 2012, Australia
enquiries@currency.com.au
www.currency.com.au

Introduction © Kate Mulvany 2009; *Home* © PP Cranney; *The Yum Yum Room* © Stephen House; *Crowded House* © John Romeril; *The Bridge* © Chris Thompson

Reprinted 2021.

COPYING FOR EDUCATIONAL PURPOSES
The Australian *Copyright Act 1968* (Act) allows a maximum of one chapter or 10% of this book, whichever is the greater, to be copied by any educational institution for its educational purposes provided that that educational institution (or the body that administers it) has given a remuneration notice to Copyright Agency (CA) under the Act. For details of the CA licence for educational institutions contact CA, 11/66 Goulburn Street, Sydney NSW 2000; Ph 1800 066 844; email info@copyright.com.au

COPYING FOR OTHER PURPOSES
Except as permitted under the Act, for example a fair dealing for the purposes of study, research, criticism or review, no part of this book may be reproduced, stored in a retrieval system, or transmitted in any form or by any means without prior written permission. All enquiries should be made to the publisher at the address above.

Any performance or public reading of *Home*, *The Yum Yum Room*, *Crowded House* or *The Bridge* is forbidden unless a licence has been received from the author or the author's agent. The purchase of this book in no way gives the purchaser the right to perform the play in public, whether by means of a staged production or a reading. All applications for public performance should be addressed to the author/s, c/- Currency Press.

Typeset by Emma Vine for Currency Press.
Printed by Fineline Print + Copy Services, Revesby, NSW.
Cover design by Emma Vine.
Cover photography by Gal Mamalya / Flickr (Getty Images).

Publication of this title was assisted by the Commonwealth Government through the Australia Council, its arts funding and advisory body.

A catalogue record for this book is available from the National Library of Australia

Contents

v   HOME IS WHERE THE HEART IS?
Kate Mulvany

1   HOME
PP Cranney

55   THE YUM YUM ROOM
Stephen House

87   CROWDED HOUSE
John Romeril

127   THE BRIDGE
Chris Thompson

Home is Where the Heart Is?

Kate Mulvany

> Construed as turf, home just seems a provisional claim, a designation you make upon a place, not one it makes on you. A certain set of buildings, a glimpsed, smudged window-view across a schoolyard, a musty aroma sniffed behind a garage when you were a child, all of which come crowding in upon your latter-day senses—those are pungent things and vivid, even consoling. But to me they are also inert and nostalgic and unlikely to connect you to the real, to that essence art can sometimes achieve, which is permanence.
>
> Writer, Richard Ford

Never was a more apt statement made than in connection with the four plays presented within the pages of this new fabulous new anthology of Australian work for young adults.

Indeed, on first glance, they conform to Ford's notion of home as a 'provisional claim'. The characters plant their metaphorical flags in all manner of places—a crowded house, a refugee camp, the streets, a bridge, the suburbs of a city, a beat-up car, the nooks and crannies of a country town. From the suburban mayhem of western-Sydney to the Blue Lake of Mount Gambier, these characters have well and truly 'designated their place', and, more often than not, they do not like it. Just as Ford observes, these people have latched onto these 'homes'—through necessity, through boredom, through just not knowing anything else—but the homes have not necessarily reciprocated the favour. The 'certain set of buildings' have become dilapidated and unwelcoming, the 'glimpsed, smudged window-view' is no longer just across a single schoolyard but across entire communities tarnished with bigotry and arrogance, fear and mistrust. The 'musty aroma' comes from the decay of family breakdown, betrayed friends—and the 'pungent, vivid, consoling' memories of our childhood are tarnished by the politics of our adult life.

Fortunately, the four playwrights in this collection—John Romeril, PP Cranney, Chris Thompson and Stephen House—have also recognised the importance of allowing a home to find its owner, and it is this theme that prevails through all four of these plays. They have completely done away with any inert nostalgia and instead taken the notions of home, refuge and love and woven them beautifully into four important stories.

In *Crowded House*, John Romeril takes us to a world reminiscent of Nazi Germany, Stalinist Russia and even, yes—Bush's 'USOFA'—but it is ultimately our own apocalyptic backyard of Australia he is exploring.

> NEIGHBOUR: I'm not signing that.
> WILL: The neighbours didn't like us.
> NEIGHBOUR: We want their kind out of there.
> WILL: Didn't want us in institutions, didn't want us in houses either.
> NEIGHBOUR: They're driving property values down.
> WILL: Crowded house.
> RITA: He's off again.
> WILL: Crowded house.
> MORG: He'll come back to us.
> WILL: Sooner or later. Generation after generation. Everyone living in this house gets it in the neck.

Shifting from terrifying to irreverent, from heartbreaking silences to extraordinary outpourings of song, this play is an example of the 'permanence' Ford spoke of: in this case, the permanence of war—the scars that remain long after a battle is fought—be they scars of a nation, a body or a mind. As the characters search for a place in their 'crowded house' their scars—pock-marked and 'schizted out' become all the more familiar and their animalistic fight for survival and sanctuary becomes, well… very, very human.

And so we love them.

PP Cranney, in *Home* is himself a master of manipulation. His clever use of scene juxtaposition has us shaking our heads pityingly at Australia's own refugee crisis… whilst in the very next breath has us cringing shamefully in recognition of our own comfortable existences.

Speaker five says of their 'home': 'I think it's just a matter of getting used to the new place. But because it's rented—it's kind of hard. Because if I get settled in this room and then I move, there's no point in getting settled in it now.'

Speaker one follows soon after with: 'I've got photos on the wall, on the mirrors… I've got photos, like, of old friends and stuff, even though I'm not friends with some people, I still keep them up there. I'd definitely take them with me when I leave.'

Then we hear from refugee Merinda:

> This place is plagued by cholera, TB, gastroenteritis and other diseases. There is a constant lack of food and water. It is summer, the temperature is often thirty-eight degrees. We understand one thing only: we want to get out of here. We will sign anything.

When we hear someone like Merinda tell us they have watched their loved ones slaughtered in the street, the words 'I've got photos, like, of old friends and stuff…' seem breathtakingly inane.

But before we can blame the system, the government, cry out that it's out of our control, Cranney introduces us to Sam, the victim of an abusive suburban Australian household and out on the streets with her transsexual friend, Peta, and Carmen, a single mum living in her Ford with a newborn baby.

CARMEN: We had some unwanted visitors a bit earlier. I tell ya, there's some bad 'uns out tonight. Be careful. Real hoons. Out to cause trouble. Pyromaniacs. They tried to set the car on fire.

SAM: With you and Harrison inside it?

PETA: Not much fun for them otherwise. Anybody can set alight an empty vehicle.

CARMEN: See down there—a little pile of leaves and rubbish under the back tyre? They were trying to light that. They almost had it going. They'd poured some metho on it… Must've pinched it off some poor old bastard. I hope they didn't torch him, too.

SAM: I feel sick!

CARMEN: Anyway, they got a bit of flame going, but I threw some wet nappies on it—that put the dampeners on it. Pissed them right off. They started trying to kick the windows in—so I jumped out the other side and started chucking more dirty nappies at them, real shitty ones. They took off like I dunno what. They say opposites attract, and things that are alike repel. They were repelled alright. But they were a mean-looking pair. In from the suburbs, I reckon, out to cause trouble. So be careful out tonight, okay? Be real careful.

SAM: Do you want us to call the cops?
CARMEN: Nah, I got plenty more shitty nappies. Besides, bad enough the locals ringing the cops all the time and complaining about me.

And in one fell swoop, Cranney gets us again. Suddenly our doors seemed *too* locked, our possessions *too* material, our minds *too* closed, and we are left pondering the child growing up in a Ford Falcon or the young mother with cholera who has no choice of whether he or she 'gets settled in or not'.

It is not sledgehammer writing—Cranney is too clever for that. There is no finger-pointing, no blame, no twisting of facts—Cranney writes with an honesty and keen observational eye that manages to not only make us love ourselves and our creature comforts a little less, but start to love the people outside a little more.

Love intermingles profoundly with refuge in Chris Thompson's *The Bridge*. This AWGIE-winning play deserves its accolades. Without a skerrick of sentimentality, Thompson explores the intricacies of love in a small town—love between mother and father, father and son, aunt and nephew, friend and enemy. Thompson beautifully explores the notion of being able to love someone and hate them all at once, and uses this boiling pot of emotion to allow his characters to seek refuge in the most heartbreaking of places—drugs, grief, apathy, suicide. At the funeral of a friend who has committed suicide off the town bridge, Aaron cries, 'It's bullshit. I bet it's the first time Donny's ever been in a church.' In one line, Thompson reminds us that even in death, it's often other people who decide where we 'belong'. Aaron surmises that his dead friend Donny will have an eternal search for 'refuge', his hunt for 'home' is infinite. He knows this because he recognises he is on the same journey. The metaphor of its title *The Bridge* is ultimately not lost, however, and through darkness, Thompson suffuses us with light as each character finds their 'home', in heart, mind, body and community. Through love, they cross dangerous tracks to find themselves and in doing so take us with them.

The age-old (but consistently baffling) notion of love is also explored within the delicious walls of *The Yum Yum Room*. Again, we are observers of a small town—this time through the rich text of Stephen House. The search for refuge in this play is far more intricate than the literal title would suggest. Although we are introduced to an actual physical place of refuge and comfort, it works more as a suggestion of the intricacies of the play's characters. Again, each of them searching for solace—a place where they are truly allowed to be themselves. And again, love is the invisible character in this play and is wrapped around every word. Tom has been betrayed by love—his mother left him as a child to be brought up by his father. His father has accepted his love—a kind usually forbidden in small towns—but in the process has lost how to communicate his love for his son. Mrs Mac has known love many times over. She is our eyes and ears and her presence and resilience reminds us that love may break a heart but not a backbone. She is the spine of this wonderful play but, ironically, its most hard-to-reach character, Annabelle, is the one to get the most profound line, 'I wish we had somewhere we could go just together… don't you?'—a line that pretty much sums up the heart of this entire collection of plays.

It may seem pat to ask you as readers to 'look for the love' in each of this pieces, but I ask it with a cynical brain and a wry smile. The theme of love, of course, is not always roses and wine. In these four plays, love is the warped, grotty, torn and tattered map that each of the characters carries in their search for a 'place'. Whether it be the questioning love between strangers of 'what happened?' in Romeril's *Crowded House* or the dreamy love of 'What can be' between a wise old woman and an angry young man in *The Yum Yum Room*; the hardened robust love of 'what if?' in *The Bridge* or the heartbreakingly loveless 'What is' of *Home*—all have a painful but persistent pulse that is worth the journey. As Ford said so eloquently, 'home' should 'connect you to the real, to that essence art can sometimes achieve, which is permanence'. Well, with these four plays, Romeril, Cranney, Thompson and House have done just that, and after reading these plays, that essence will remain in your hearts and minds with the permanence any good home offers.

Kate Mulvany

Kate Mulvany is a playwright and an actor. She is the recipient of the Philip Parsons Young Playwright's Award for *The Danger Age*. Her other plays include *The Seed* and *The Web*.

Home
PP Cranney

PP CRANNEY started writing professionally in the late seventies in Sydney for cabaret and pub theatre. He has since written for theatre companies, community organisations, government and corporate enterprises all over Australia. He has over thirty years experience as a freelance writer for stage, particularly for youth and community theatre, as well as for children's television, short film, radio and corporate video.

He has had eight plays nominated for Australian Writers' Guild AWGIE awards and has twice won an AWGIE Award: in 1999, for *Rated X*, and in 2001, for *Home*.

In 2003 he received a Centenary Medal for services to Australian society in writing for the stage.

Seeking refuge: in the 2000 Shopfront Theatre production, refugees flee their war-torn homelands. (Photograph courtesy of Shopfront Theatre)

Home was first produced by Shopfront Theatre for Young People at Shopfront Theatre, Carlton, on 6 October 2000 with the following cast:

DOMOVOI	Christopher Sargant
MERINDA	Anna Slowiacek
ALI	Shanoah Halpin
MOTHER/NEWSREADER	Shiereen Magsalin
TEACHER	Sarah Abaron
TONY	Kevin Bowen
MAN IN BARRACKS/GUARD	Steve Simao
POLITICIAN	Sally Williams
SAM	Rhiannon Smith
MUM'S VOICE/MR SLEAZE	Bonnie McKenzie
JO	Amanda Wormald
PETA/GUARD	Nicholas Slowiacek
RANGER/OCKER	Rosie Catalano
CARMEN/OFFICIAL	Jacqui Singh
CHRISSIE/COMMANDER	Heather Scott
LISA	Jackie Turner
BILLY/GUARD	Khye McCann
SUBURBAN STORIES	Rosie Catalano, Sarah Abaron, Sally Williams, Shiereen Magsalin, Jacqui Singh, Heather Scott, Melanie Isaacs, Jackie Turner, Nicholas Slowiacek, Kevin Bowen

All other roles were performed by the company.

Directors, Melinda Collie-Holmes and Sahraya Stewart
Designer, Imogen Ross
Musical Director, TJ Eckleberg
Movement Director, Anastasia Wong-Perera
Lighting Designer, Martin Kinnane
Costume Designer, Cindy Rodriguez
Production Manager, Annie McNamara

Home was commissioned by Shopfront Theatre for Young People, Carlton NSW, and researched and workshopped in collaboration with the cast.

CHARACTERS

DOM, a domovoi, appears in all three storylines.

HOMELAND:
MERINDA
ALI
MOTHER
BORDER GUARD 1
BORDER GUARD 2
EMBASSY OFFICIAL
INTEPRETER
OCKER MAN
TEACHER
TONY
POLITICIAN
REFUGEES, OFFICIALS,
MEDIA, STUDENTS

SAM:
SAM
MUM
JO
MR SLEAZE
PETA
HOMELESS MEN
RANGER
CARMEN
HOON 1
HOON 2
CHRISSIE
LISA
BILLY

IN THE SUBURBS:
5 TEENAGERS
MUM
PARENTS
HOMELESS PERSON
LADY
BUS DRIVER

SETTING

The stories in *Home* are held together by a displaced Domovoi (Slavic house spirit), who guides us through a space that must represent many locations including a war-torn village, a refugee camp, a suburban house, a flat, an inner-city park, back lanes and squats.

ACT ONE

PROLOGUE

Unearthly lights and thunder build up an expectation of the entrance of some fantastic mythical creature. After a few moments, anticlimactically, DOM *the domovoi appears from the packing cases. He steps forward to address the audience.*

DOM: In the beginning, God created the heavens and the earth. And the earth became home to a multitude of species—including humans, such as yourselves. And when the creator had finished creating the heavens and the earth, some of the spirits who surrounded him revolted against him. And he drove these rebellious spirits from the sky and cast them to earth below. Many of those spirits fell into the water or the forests and remained wicked, but some of us fell onto the roofs of people's houses, and through mixing with you humans, we became good spirits—a little cheeky and mischievous at times, perhaps, but basically good.

We domovoi made ourselves so much at home in the homes of you humans. We became house spirits, little divinities of home and hearth.

But please note: we weren't freeloaders or anything like that. We paid our way: we forewarned you when troubles threatened. Eh? We'd tug the missus' hair when hubby was about to beat her. That's got to be worth something. And before the death of a family member, we wept. We're only human. Well, we're not humans, not yet, but we have feelings too. We loved living near the stove or under the front doorstep. We appreciated the occasional slice of bread slipped under the stove; mention our names in the house, and we'd always bring happiness to your home.

But that was then, this is now: isn't it ironic? The master of the house is now himself homeless. And why is this? Humans don't believe in what's important anymore. Nowadays, you believe not in goblins, but in globalisation! Not in pixies, but profits! Not magic, but money! There is no room in your hearts and imaginations for household divinities.

So I am forced to learn to become human, so that I might find myself a human home. But right now I find myself in the middle of human conflict!

The scene becomes a war zone.

Ha, the twentieth century—such a schmozzle! World wars, cold wars, star wars, trade wars, holy wars, crusades, jihads, civil wars—sheesh!

You trying to wreck this planet or what? If I were your landlord I'd kick you out and keep your bond, that's what I would do.

SCENE ONE: HOMELAND 1—WAR ZONE

MERINDA *emerges from the war zone to speak to the audience.* ALI *enters behind her.*

MERINDA: Shortly after the war started, our father left our home to visit his parents in a village some distance from the city. He was to return after two days, but he did not—his parents' village fell to the army soon after he left us. We haven't heard from him for months, though it seems more like an eternity as not knowing what has happened to him—if he is alive, or killed, or tortured—plays on our minds relentlessly. I eventually lose hope and believe that he is dead.

ALI: Our father is not dead. He will return.

MERINDA: The shelling of our city continues. Many of our friends, relatives and neighbours are killed or maimed. For months, we remain in the basement of our home.

At bedtime, we never know if we will see the light of day again. Each night we bid farewell to each other rather than say goodnight, never certain that we will wake up the next morning. Food and water is scarce. There is no electricity, no communication with the outside world. I watch my mother turn into a skeleton before my very eyes.

After a long siege, our town is taken by the army. Soldiers come each day to our house to ask us where our father is. 'We don't know where he is, we haven't seen him for months.'

Dreamlike [or nightmare-like] images of Merinda's MOTHER *and her brother* ALI *being persecuted by uniformed soldiers: being pushed about, having the barrel of a gun held up to* MOTHER*'s head while* ALI *is held back by other soldiers. The soldiers push* MOTHER *to the ground and exit.* ALI *and* MERINDA *comfort* MOTHER.

It is too much to bear. One day, a cousin of ours arrives to tell us that they are leaving the city that night, and asks our mother and us to come with them.

MOTHER: I'm too sick to make the journey. But you must take Merinda.
ALI: Mother, you come with us or none of us will go.
MOTHER: I'm too sick to travel I tell you! You and your sister must go. Find somewhere safe.
ALI: [*and* CHORUS] *But the soldiers will come back.*
    Words in italics are echoed by the chorus.
MOTHER: They'll leave me alone.
ALI: But what about our Father?
MERINDA: Our father is dead, otherwise we— [would have heard from him.]
ALI: We don't know that for certain!
MOTHER: And if he is alive, I will be here when he returns. And you will be somewhere safe. That's what he would want.
ALI: No, I won't leave you here alone. I will stay here and wait for our father's return.
MOTHER: *You are old enough now for their army.* They are taking all the young men away to fight and kill their own brothers.
ALI: I won't let them take me.
MOTHER: You'll have no choice.
ALI: This is my home—I won't be driven away like some animal.
MOTHER: First you must defend your sister. She can't stay here much longer, she is not safe. *They don't only use guns against us.* Rape is their weapon, too.
MERINDA: Mum! Don't talk like this!
MOTHER: Take her away from here, protect her, look after her…
MERINDA: Mum, *we can't go without you.* Please—
ALI: I can look after you both.
MOTHER: [*to* ALI] Do you think your father would let her stay here now, the way things are? Don't worry about me.
    ALI *pulls the distressed* MERINDA *away from* MOTHER.

ALI: Go pack your bags. *One bag. And a blanket.* Only what you can carry. We'll go to our cousins just after dark. Go, now.
MERINDA: But, Mum—
MOTHER: Do as your brother says.
MERINDA: Ali, we can't leave her—
ALI: I said, *get your things, now!*

>MERINDA *leaves them.* MOTHER *takes from her pocket or purse a key on a string and hands it to* ALI.

MOTHER: Take this. The key to your home. For when you return. This war cannot last forever.
ALI: What are you talking about? You'll be here to let us in when we return.
MOTHER: [*putting the key on the string around his neck*] Please look after your sister.

>*They hug each other farewell.* MERINDA *appears with their bags, hugs her* MOTHER *farewell.* MERINDA *and* ALI *begin their journey.*
>
>DOM *picks up his gear and follows them.*

DOM: I'll go with them. Wait for me!
MERINDA: [*to the audience*] Ali and I, we walk for two days to reach the border—all the time never knowing if we would see my mother again. At the border crossing, our passports and papers seem to be in order.

>ALI *hands money over to one of two* BORDER GUARDS.

GUARD 1: This is all the money you have?
ALI: Yes! Our papers are in order, aren't they?
GUARD 1: There are fees, expenses. You go on through. She must stay.
ALI: No, she comes with me.
GUARD 1: You go, she stays—or you both stay. Unless you pay…
ALI: You have all our money. It's not fair, it can't be legal!
GUARD 2: Ha! Legal, he says! You can go on—the girl stays.
ALI: I'm not going without my sister.
GUARD 2: I know how she can pay her dues!

>*The* GUARDS *roughly begin to drag* MERINDA *away.* ALI *tries to pull them off her.*

MERINDA: Go on, Ali, get away while you can.
ALI: No, wait, we have more money—wait. We can pay.
  ALI *begins to pull some more cash out of a sock or shoe or some hidden pocket.*
GUARD 1: Let her go—they have money.
MERINDA: But Ali, we'll have nothing...
GUARD 2: But we can have the money and the girl!
GUARD 1: You think I'm as low as you are, you scum!
GUARD 2: But—
GUARD 1: We take the money or the girl. I have principles, you pig! Let her go! Get back to your post!
  GUARD 1 *takes* MERINDA'*s passport and stamps it, hands it back to her.* GUARD 2 *roughly grabs her again by the arm.*
GUARD 2: She's a scarecrow, anyway—too skinny for my taste!
GUARD 1: To your post, I said! [*To* MERINDA *and* ALI] Have a safe journey, friends! Ha, ha!
  DOM *kicks* GUARD 1 *in the behind, who then turns on* GUARD 2. Why you—!
  GUARD 1 *chases* GUARD 2 *off.*
MERINDA: Across the border, we stay in a refugee camp: overcrowded, dirty, and not much food but no shelling, no sniper fire. I miss my mother, and my father still.
  Images of MERINDA *and* ALI *with other refugees, endlessly waiting in, and being redirected to, queue after queue, filling out forms etc.*
  After many weeks, we hear some good news: we are to leave the camp.
ALI: Temporary only. In France? England? Not too far.
MERINDA: Not France, not England.
ALI: America? Canada? Not too bad, I suppose...
MERINDA: Not America. Not Canada. Australia.
ALI: Australia?
MERINDA: We have an uncle in Australia. I will write to Mum and find out where he lives. He is bound to help us.
DOM: Australia? Maybe there people will have kind and open hearts. But first—more paper work.

An EMBASSY OFFICIAL *enters, followed by* INTERPRETER.

OFFICIAL: You will come to Australia as 'displaced persons'. Special legislation. You must be clear about that. [*To* INTERPRETER] Please make sure they understand that—it's important.

INTERPRETER: You will be going to Australia as 'displaced persons'. Special Australia legislation. You understand?

ALI: [*to* INTERPRETER] But what does this mean—'displaced person'?

INTERPRETER: They want to know what it means to be a 'displaced person'—

OFFICIAL: Of course they do! I haven't finished explaining yet, have I? Let me go on. As displaced persons, you will have no rights to seek to apply to stay in Australia as refugees or migrants. No rights to do that. You must sign this agreement, this contract that says you will not seek to do that. Okay?

The INTERPRETER *has translated simultaneously.*

INTERPRETER: Do you understand what he is saying? You sign the agreement that you have no right to seek asylum as refugees. You understand?

MERINDA: [*to audience, over* INTERPRETER] This place is plagued by cholera, TB, gastroenteritis and other diseases. There is a constant lack of food and water. It is summer, the temperature is often thirty-eight degrees. We understand one thing only: we want to get out of here. We will sign anything.

She signs the agreement. ALI *is hesitant.*

We must sign.

ALI *signs.*

The EMBASSY OFFICIAL *and* INTERPRETER *exit, and* DOM *re-enters.*

DOM: What awaits us in our new homeland? As temporary as it might be. A new country, a new home, a new life…? What are we waiting for? I don't have supernatural powers for nothing—let's go!

SCENE TWO: IN THE SUBURBS 1—MORNING TIME

Morning noises fade up and morning light dawns on five young sleeping teenagers.

HOME

DOM: And here we are—in the suburbs. Hey, everybody—time to get up!

The sleepers stretch and yawn, and address the audience and/or each other, performing 'normal' morning routines. Dialogue overlaps and speeches interweave where appropriate.

TEENAGER 1: When my mum comes home from work, she taps on my window, so I can open the door, and, yeah, so like I wake up…

TEENAGER 2: At quarter to seven by my alarm, but I can't get up until seven o'clock—like I need that fifteen minutes of just lying there doing nothing.

TEENAGER 1: She works the midnight shift for her nursing home, but my keys went missing…

TEENAGER 4: At eleven o'clock—eleven or twelve—because I don't go to school, and I have plenty time.

TEENAGER 1: And so I took hers, so she doesn't have a house key, like, 'cos she doesn't go out anyway, so she has to tap on the window.

TEENAGER 3: Mum makes noises in the kitchen when she's putting away dishes and stuff… And then I kind of lie in bed, half-awake, dreading school for about an hour…

TEENAGER 5: I leave the blinds open, so that usually wakes me up. I don't like clocks and stuff… I just get up when I want. Well, my cat wakes me up; she gets up and meows at me, to be fed and to go out. I want to sleep in like you [TEENAGER 4] till eleven or ten; it's much more natural. But I think I sleep too much, I think.

TEENAGER 4: I love sleeping so much. I sleep like a little baby.

TEENAGER 5: I've heard that, like, twelve hours is too much sleep… But everyone's different.

TEENAGER 1: Dogs barking… television… Cow'n'chicken cartoons…

TEENAGER 2: Pretty quiet, apart from the radio—Triple J—it's mine and my mother's choice.

TEENAGER 3: Triple J, Mum's footsteps, dishes.

TEENAGER 2: My mother's weird—she loves grunge music. At least I don't have to listen to Celine Dion or some crap like that.

TEENAGER 1: And my brother's music. He's got turntables, sometimes he's on them before school, practising. He's a DJ, at least he's trying to be, so there's a lot of stupid mixes.

TEENAGER 2: One more sound: my dog barking—he's a little tiny

Jack Russell-cross-Chihuahua-thing, and all he does is bark at everything, and my cat stands there screaming—Meahh! Meahh! Meooow!

TEENAGER 3: Then I make breakfast which could either be toast or cereal…

TEENAGER 2: Mum wants me to eat breakfast even though she doesn't like it herself, but I never do. She tells me that I should, like, saying:

MUM: Have some toast, have some cereal.

TEENAGER 2: I don't want any! She gave up—she knows I'm not going to eat it. Every now and then she still tries to make me, but she just pretty much has given up.

TEENAGER 1: Because I've got an Indian background, usually, my mum makes curry or something for my dad in the morning…

TEENAGER 2: I used to eat breakfast ages ago but now it makes me sick—I don't know why. One day I had breakfast and I was walking to school and I felt really sick, and then I felt sick all day.

TEENAGER 1: Dad loves curry. I suppose he's been brought up like that, but I don't like curry much… I usually have, like, tea or toast, or sometimes cereal.

TEENAGER 2: Sometimes I have coffee or tea or Milo or orange juice, but that's all I'll have.

TEENAGER 4: Actually, my mum, she always makes breakfast for me. Yeah, always. Not my brothers. Just me. I'm her little baby…

TEENAGER 5: I just drink water. I eat at the office.

TEENAGER 4: I just have breakfast with my mum, we talk a little bit about everything, and afterwards we go shopping. Every day, every day because I don't have any other obligations, so…

TEENAGER 1: I go to the bathroom, do my thing, get into my school clothes, stand in front of the heater, and go outside, see the dogs—they're usually barking by this stage.

TEENAGER 3: I prepare my school stuff, like my bag and my books and all that. Then I get dressed and do my hair. Altogether it takes about twenty-five minutes, but this takes, like, lots of walking out and talking to Mum for a bit, if she's still awake.

TEENAGER 2: Usually I'm in a rush to get to school, but if she gets up in time—because I normally get up before her—if she's up in time…

TEENAGER 1: Before I leave the house I tell my mum whether or not I'm going to be late, even though she's still half asleep…

TEENAGER 2: We talk a bit, like, she'll ask me what I've got today, like what classes, or if I have to do anything after school, and then she complains about people at work and stuff, and I complain about school and then I just go.

TEENAGER 3: I kind of hang around until eight when the news on Triple J comes on and then—

TEENAGER 5: I'm supposed to be at work at about nine, but I usually I get there about quarter to ten… No-one seems to notice. I'm just in an office.

TEENAGER 3: I kind of just brush my teeth, walk to the bus stop where, like, all the clever, cool kids bitch about, like, parties they just went to and got drunk at and threw up and stuff—

TEENAGER 4: And when I come back home with my mum, we make some lunch, together.

TEENAGER 3: It's the whole kinda scene-group thing, and they talk about how they got drunk and how cool it is and stuff…

TEENAGER 5: Like I love sleeping and I'm in my deepest feeling when I sleep, but getting up it's like 'Oh, God!'

TEENAGER 3: Another day!

TEENAGER 5: I'm always in a bad mood when I wake up I always feel crap when I wake up, I just think, 'Oh shit—

ALL: Another day.

They exit.

SCENE THREE: SAM 1—RUNAWAY

DOM: Yes, another day—I think I'm gonna like it here! So peaceful and quiet, no noise of battling and fighting and—

The sound of a domestic argument cuts him off. Enter 15-year-old girl, SAM, *and her* MUM, *fighting.*

SAM: Why can't I?

MUM: Because I'm your mother and I say so.

SAM: It's not fair. You're always doing this to me—on purpose.

MUM: Don't talk rubbish, you stupid girl.

SAM: Yeah, it's always stupid Sam, stupid girl. That's what you get for having a stupid mother.

MUM: I'll slap your mouth if you don't shut up, you cheeky little bitch.

SAM: Yeah, you would too—while Dad's not round.

> MUM *slaps* SAM.

Ahh! You bitch!
MUM: You want another one—just try me.
SAM: I hate you, I hate you, I hate you!
MUM: Get out of my house, you ungrateful little slut.
SAM: Fuck you.

> *The fight continues and other sounds of domestic violence—shouting and crying, doors slamming and objects being thrown—become increasingly loud. The noise becomes over the top, surreal.*

DOM: Hey, hey, language, language! Such a nice, leafy, sunny suburb—what's to fight about?

> DOM *follows* SAM, *with her bag packed, as she approaches her younger sister* JO, *who is upset after the mighty row.* SAM *puts her hand on* JO's *shoulder—*JO *shrugs it off.*

JO: Leave me alone.
SAM: I'm sorry. She starts it all the time.
JO: I hate it.
SAM: Well, there won't be any more.
JO: What do you mean?
SAM: What do you reckon?
JO: No, please don't go. She doesn't mean it—she can't help it.
SAM: It doesn't matter. I can't stand it any more. Now listen, you're not to tell Mum a thing, okay? You didn't see where I went, okay?
JO: But where are you going? I wanna come too.
SAM: Get real.
JO: Don't leave me here with her.
SAM: What are you worried about? You're the baby, the favourite. She loves you, you'll be cool. Enjoy it while you can.
JO: It's not my fault.
SAM: Sshhhh. I know, I know. Listen, I've got my mobile—there's a month left, anyway, prepaid. You can always call me.
JO: And you can call here.
SAM: No way. *She* might answer.
JO: But a month? You'll come back home before then, won't you?

SAM: Might have a new home by then… You go back to bed, okay? Go on, good night.

    JO *exits.* SAM *watches her go, then exits.*

MUM: [*off stage*] Sam? Sam, are you out there?

DOM: Sam? Sam, where are you going? Oh, dear! Not to worry, this is not the only suburb in town. Come with me…

SCENE FOUR: HOMELAND 2—BARRACKS

In Australia, the displaced persons arrive at their 'Safe haven'. As DOM *delivers his spiel, the ensemble creates the feel of the barracks, arriving, and queuing, being directed by* OFFICIALS, *unpacking their bags, etc.*

DOM: This way… Welcome to a little bit of Australian suburbia tourists seldom get a chance to see. Built by a bend in the river and set in pleasant bush surrounds, this late 50s complex offers its guests complete privacy and seclusion—you wouldn't know it was here unless you drove right up to the front gate. Ideal from a security point of view. The central feature of this charming hideaway is a double-storey grey besser brick building offering good motel-style accommodation, very reasonable compared to some other—well, compared to the other old army barracks on offer. Yes, these barracks make an ideal haven for our international visitors, our displaced persons. I do hope Merinda and Ali make the best of their new home away from home…

MERINDA: [*to audience*] Many tears are shed in those first days in this new country where everything—the language, the food, the customs—everything is so different. At least families are not separated. They push their single beds together to make one big bed, so that they sleep in together, to feel safe, to give each other comfort and strength.

ALI: Don't worry. We'll be safe enough here—for a while. I'll look after you.

MERINDA: [*to audience*] Not long after we arrive, there is controversy. Back home, a man has piggybacked his old and frail mother for four whole days across the mountains to reach the refugee camp. When finally they bring him and his family to Australia, he realises his mother is incontinent. But the barracks where they send them are a long way from here, out of the city.

MAN: There are no toilets in the rooms—they are half a kilometre away. My mother must walk across maybe six, seven times a night, sometimes it is minus five degrees.

MERINDA: We've just come from a hot, hot summer.

MAN: And the showers have no partitions—there is no privacy.

MERINDA: He 'causes trouble', refuses to obey orders. Returning from an outing, he refuses to get off the bus.

The MAN *and* HIS MOTHER *refuse to move at the request of frustrated officials. The* MEDIA *with cameras and microphones begin to surround them.*

MAN: I'm not trying to cause any trouble. My duty is to care for my mother and my family. I can't subject her to this humiliation! Please—

MERINDA: In the end they were brought back here to our barracks. But people, even our own people, read things in the newspaper.

Headlines such as 'REFUGEES REFUSE ACCOMODATION—NOT GOOD ENOUGH, THEY SAY' are shown to the audience.

REFUGEE 1: [*to the* MAN] You can't behave like that—you bring shame on all of us!

REFUGEE 2: We should be grateful to Australia—no complaining!

Enter OCKER.

OCKER: Can you friggin' believe those friggin' whingeing bloody reffoes! For Crissake, we bring 'em out here, give 'em friggin' decent food and shelter, at our expense, with our friggin' taxpayers money. We save 'em from friggin' killing themselves in their own friggin' war-torn mongrel country, and all they can friggin' do is complain about conditions here! Jesus Christ! Fuck me dead, I'm so sorry we can't afford to friggin' put you all up at the friggin' Hilton friggin' Hotel! I mean, fair friggin' dinkum, can you friggin' believe that?! If it were up to me, I'd friggin' send the whole friggin' pack of 'em back to where they all friggin' well come from! And good friggin' riddance!

The MAN *and* HIS MOTHER *are escorted off stage.*

MERINDA: The man, his mother and his family were deported—back to the refugee camps we had escaped from.
OCKER: Yeah, and serves 'em bloody well right too, friggin' ungrateful bastards!

SCENE FIVE: IN THE SUBURBS 2—MY ROOM

TEENAGER 4: I've got a room in the roof. My dad made that for me—so if I have a fight with them, or something, it's like my own little world up there, and no-one goes up there…

TEENAGER 1: My room? It's… it's like… mine. I mean, they can still come in whenever they like, but they mainly just leave me alone… So…

TEENAGER 2: It's nice not to be reminded: it's their house, you abide by their rules. It's their telephone, their food, their clothes that are on your back and basically 'This room's mine not yours so piss off!'

TEENAGER 3: Because there's so many people in my house, and it's never quiet. It's like, I'm hardly ever by myself at home…

TEENAGER 2: There's no locks or anything, but they know that if the door's closed that they can't come in, because I'll abuse them. I'll totally abuse them.

TEENAGER 3: I used to just go down a few blocks and go to like this circuit place, where people with their Ls, they usually just practise driving and stuff, and I'd just sit there for a while.

TEENAGER 5: In my old house I used to have a bedroom, and then I had, like, a playroom upstairs. I didn't really spend much time in the rest of the house—it was either my playroom or the bedroom. That was it. But now that we've moved, I don't have anything.

TEENAGER 6: When I lived at home, I had a granny flat which was separated from the house. It was pretty scungy, but it had its own bathroom, and it was pretty big. So that was cool 'cos I had—I could lock the doors.

TEENAGER 1: I don't have any posters or anything because I'm going to be moving anyway. Yeah. And then I'm going to decorate.

TEENAGER 2: Pink flowers?

TEENAGER 1: Oh yes—sunshine and lollipops and stuff. No, something really really funky and abstract.

TEENAGER 5: My old bedroom was messy, but it was safe. Like, I had this mural on my wall which my dad painted when I was seven. And it was like Rainbow Brite and this castle and Bambi and I really really loved it, because that was my wall.

TEENAGER 6: Rainbow... who?

TEENAGER 5: Rainbow Brite.

TEENAGER 2: Wasn't that the bitch in the rainbow colours?!

TEENAGER 5: She was nice!

TEENAGER 4: I love my room. My room is just the bestest room in world. It has no door, it has a curtain. It has absolutely no windows, so it's pitch black in the middle of the day, so you can sleep whenever you want. I'm allowed to paint it any colour I want, I can do anything I want up there.

TEENAGER 3: I'm not really concerned with decorating my room, because I'm hardly ever home anyway.

TEENAGER 5: I used to have a mirror on the back of my old door, so every time I close my door I expect there to be a mirror, but it's not there. So it just doesn't feel the same. And my mum's got all of upstairs, you know, that's her territory, and my dad's got all of downstairs. It's a garage.

TEENAGER 2: You've got the backyard!

TEENAGER 5: No, that's for the dog.

TEENAGER 2: You've got the front yard?

TEENAGER 5: No, that's for the car. So I've got Roselands Shopping Centre. I could go there. Woohoo!

TEENAGER 5: I think it's just a matter of getting used to the new place. But because it's rented—it's kind of hard. Because if I get settled in this room and then I move, there's no point in getting settled in it now.

TEENAGER 6: That was a pretty cool room, because it was completely separate from the house, so I could do whatever I want. I had to crank the music up pretty loud before Mum and Dad would hear it in the house.

TEENAGER 5: My walls used to be completely covered with posters when I was going through that poster thing when you cover your walls completely in all posters, and movies stars and all that. And then I took it all down because I didn't like that anymore...

TEENAGER 6: They had a key, but they kind've knew, well, they knew if the door was locked, but. They still considered it theirs, and they still barged in no matter when—and that got, yuck. They came in when they shouldn't've one time, so...

TEENAGER 5: And now I just have pictures of the shows I've been in and the posters... And I have little pictures of my friends and the things that I've done.

TEENAGER 3: About the locks thing—I've got heaps of locks on my door. Yeah, no-one's allowed in my room. Basically, everyone in the house has locks on their door, because we had, like, problems before, and stuff.

TEENAGER 1: I've got photos on the wall, on the mirrors... I've got photos, like, of old friends and stuff, even though I'm not friends with some people, I still keep them up there. I'd definitely take them with me when I leave.

TEENAGER 3: Yeah. Posters. I used to have heaps of posters everywhere with, like, bands and stuff... But now I've got just this big Live poster, because when I met them and they signed it.

TEENAGER 6: My room is my room because it's got all those parts of my life, and all that history of my life.

TEENAGER 2: I'll probably take everything off... Take it to my new place and start all over again. It's sort of like a step thing. Like, that was one thing, now I'm going to move on to something different.

TEENAGER 4: I'm planning on getting a humungous truck and lifting my room to a little block of land and putting my room there.

TEENAGER 2: I've always had this dream... I always had this dream that I was lying in my bed, I would press a button, the floor would open up and my bed would just slide down and go 'shank!' into this secret area. A cave—a bat cave. I've always wanted a bat cave, and have like—all these stalactite, stalagmite, things—you know what I'm talking about? They hang off the roof. And people would just go 'Argh! Argh!' and I'd be like 'Ha ha ha.' And make all these magic things happen. It's like... ohh! It's my dream. To own a bat cave.

SCENE SIX: SAM 2—MR SLEAZE

SAM *enters a park, sits on a bench. She is clearly nervous. As she sits there in the dark, it gradually becomes apparent that there are people in sleeping bags and cardboard boxes settling in for the night.*

DOM *follows her.*

DOM: Oh, Sam, what are we doing out here alone like this? I don't feel safe…

> DOM *tugs at her hair, but she shrugs him away like a mozzie.* MR SLEAZE *enters.*

MR SLEAZE: [*to audience*] Tasty, tasty, very tasty… Just how I like 'em—young and vulnerable. Ha, ha, ha! [*To* SAM] Er… hello there.

DOM: This guy's trouble. I warned her but would she listen? I'd better go get some help.

> DOM *exits.* SAM *ignores* MR SLEAZE *till his intentions become obvious. She tries to move away but he blocks her.*

MR SLEAZE: I say, hello there. You don't have any cigarettes, do you?

He offers her a cigarette and SAM *shakes her head to his offer.*

Yeah, that's good, you don't want to smoke at your age. Smoking's bad for you, bad for your health. [*He coughs.*] I'm going to give the bloody things up myself one day.

I say, nice night, eh? For winter. A nice winter's night. Bit chilly, though, don't you think? Eh? You must be a bit chilly in that get up? Looks a bit flimsy, are you sure you're warm enough? I could help warm you up if you like… I mean, don't get me wrong, about what you're wearing, like, it's very attractive, shows off your figure nicely. You've got a very nice figure, if you don't mind me saying so. What are you up to, anyway? I mean, would you like to earn a little bit of cash, a bit of cash money? Would that warm you up, a little bit of extra cash money on a chilly winter's night… ?

Hey, hey, hey, don't be shy, no need to play hard to get, I've got the cash, got the cash on me, no worries about that… You have to earn it of course, but it wouldn't be hard—well it will be hard, ha, ha! You're very pretty. You've got a very pretty mouth. Would you mind if I kissed you? Come on, give us a kiss.

SAM *resists.*

I see, I see. Business first, eh? Not just a pretty face. How much, how much? Twenty bucks? Thirty bucks? Just quick, just quick. Thirty bucks and you touch me, touch me, touch me, down there, you'll like it, you'll like it—you should be paying me! Thirty bucks for a hand job. More where that comes from. Fifty bucks for French? You've got a beautiful mouth, pretty lips. Put 'em down there… fifty dollars, eh? Sixty dollars? No more than that—I can get the works down the road for eighty bucks. You want eighty bucks? You got somewhere to go? You got a room?

SAM: No, no leave me alone—let me go.

MR SLEAZE: Talkative now, found your tongue, eh? I thought the cat had your tongue there for a minute… But it's a lovely tongue, a lovely mouth. Put it down here, go on, put it down here …

SAM: No, no, no. Leave me alone—

MR SLEAZE: You like it a little bit rough? Eh? That's okay, just shut up, okay, shut up!

> SAM *is struggling to get away from* MR SLEAZE. PETA, *a transsexual, is escorted in by* DOM.

PETA Hey, you—hey, little-dick, leave her alone. She said no, she means no.

MR SLEAZE: Piss off, you queer bitch.

PETA: If you can't read her lips, read mine: Fuck off! [*She hits him.*] Get away from her before I call the police!

> MR SLEAZE *exits.*

Are you alright, love?

SAM: Thank you, thank you very much—I don't know how I can repay you.

PETA: You don't have any cigarettes, do you?

SCENE SEVEN: HOMELAND 3—ENGLISH LESSONS

In a classroom, about half a dozen students, including ALI, MERINDA *and her new girlfriends, are at an English class. It is very much a beginner's introductory class, starting with names. When* MERINDA *and* ALI *talk between themselves in their first language they are fluent. Speaking English, they are less so.*

TEACHER: My first name is Maree. What is your first name?

STUDENT 1: Er… my first name is Maree.

A couple of the other STUDENTS *start laughing, joined by the others as they realise the mistake. One of the* STUDENTS *whispers to* STUDENT 1, *who herself laughs with embarrassment. The* TEACHER *laughs along with them.* ALI *is the only one who seems not to be enjoying the class.*

TEACHER: It's alright, don't worry. Settle down. Let's try again: *My first name is Maree.* What is *your* first name?

STUDENT 1: My… name first—

TEACHER: My first name.

STUDENT 1: First name is… Liridona.

TEACHER: Very good. Liridona. What a pretty name. Now all of us will say: 'Good morning Liridona'.

CLASS: Good morning, Liridona.

MERINDA: [*to audience*] English is not so easy to learn, but I'm throwing myself into learning it. Ali is still very depressed, thinking only of when we can return to our homeland. It was hard to get him to come to the English class.

ALI: What's the use? We won't be here long enough to use the language. We will be going home soon.

MERINDA: We don't know that. If we learn to speak, we can leave the barracks more often. Go out more. Find work. Have fun.

ALI: Fun!

MERINDA: You mope around here all day as if you're in some prison camp. I want to go out—with my new friends. They tell us this: it is not a prison here—we are free to come and go as we please. They tell us, respect this place like it's our home. For now, this is our home.

ALI: This is not my home. It may as well be a prison for all I care.

MERINDA: Mum will write soon—with the address of our Uncle maybe. We might go and live with him, on the outside. We'll need English on the outside.

ALI: Outside's worse than inside—I've learnt enough English, eh? 'Reffo', 'whinger', 'bastards', eh? At least we're among our own people here.

MERINDA: Ali, please, come to the class. For my sake.

ALI: Yeah, for your sake. It's for your sake I'm in this stupid country in the first place.

MERINDA *returns to her seat in the class.* ALI *is upset and sullenly returns to his seat.* TEACHER *looks at* ALI; *it is his turn for introductions.*

TEACHER: My first name is Maree. What is your first name?

ALI *just shrugs, refusing to answer. Some of the girls in the class try to egg him on.*

GIRLS: [*whispering and giggling*] Ali, go on, Ali, tell her…

TEACHER: It's alright. Nobody has to answer if they don't feel like it. Everyone learns at their own pace. We'll move along. [*To next student*] My name is—

ALI: I know my name: my name is Ali. My name is Ali. Thank you, good morning. Thank you. Goodbye.

MERINDA *stands, upset and embarrassed by her brother. She has a flashback and the scene becomes a remembered war zone.*

MERINDA: [*to audience*] Back home, both Ali and I are very good students. He wants to study to be an engineer. Me, I'd like to be a doctor. Or a teacher. Or a singer—a pop star. When the war starts, it is harder to get to school. Mainly we go when the shelling seems to have stopped for a while. Once a sniper's bullet passed by Ali's ear by only inches. He's frightened and shocked. I try to make him feel better, make him laugh. I was walking behind him, and I tell him that I saw the bullet go in one ear and come out the other—nothing in between to stop it. But as things get worse, Ali and I can only attend classes a few days a month, and so we study at home when we can concentrate—but it is difficult when shelling occurs twenty-four hours non-stop. And all too often we hear the news that another one of our friends from school has been killed.

War zone memory fades out. MERINDA *finds that the* TEACHER *is talking to her.*

TEACHER: My first name is Maree. What is your first name?

SCENE EIGHT: SAM 3—PETA

In the park. SAM *and* PETA *on the bench.*

PETA: So what's your name, sweetie?
SAM: Sam. What's yours?

PETA: What do you think? Priscilla, of course.
SAM: Really!
PETA: No. Peta. Peta with an 'a.' You sure you don't have a cigarette on you?
SAM: No.
PETA: No, you don't have a cigarette, or no, you're not sure?
SAM: I don't smoke.
PETA: Of course not! What am I thinking? How old are you, darling?
SAM: Er, fif—f—eighteen.
PETA: Did you say fay-teen? Fay-teen? Way too young to smoke. What a wonderful age to be. I don't think I ever turned fay-teen. At least, I don't remember my fay-teenth birthday. Ah, so that's where it all went wrong.
SAM: I'm sixteen.
PETA: Sure, but a lady's never too young to start lying about her age.
SAM: I'm fifteen, alright?
PETA: Ha! [*Singing*] She is fifteen going on fayteen—la, la, la, la, la...
SAM: Are you mad or something?
PETA: What a question—what a rude question, what an extremely and extraordinarily rude and impertinent question.
SAM: I'm sorry.
PETA: Mad, bad, and dangerous to know. At least until my medication kicks in.

In the darkness around them is a group of HOMELESS MEN *sleeping, or trying to. One of them calls out.*

HOMELESS PERSON 1: I'll kick you in if ya don't shut up! I'm trying to sleep.
VOICES: Shut up? Shut up yourself!

The voices fade out.

SAM: I didn't see all those men. Are they all... homeless?
PETA: Homeless? They have the park, the streets, [*Singing*] 'the starry skies above, don't fence us in.'
VOICES: SHUT UP!
PETA: So, they—we!—can't be homeless, if this is our home. For the moment anyway. But it's not really a place for a young girl like

yourself, a mere fay-teen year old. Not that any of them would hurt you—though there are always bad apples in every barrel. It's just that someone with your tender sensibilities might find the environment a little… coarse, shall we say?

There is the sound of an enormously loud fart—a mighty raspberry that rips the still night air asunder. There are lots of groaning complaints, and some laughter.

HOMELESS PERSON 1: Christ, who dropped their guts!
HOMELESS PERSON 2: Some bastard over here—phew!
HOMELESS PERSON 3: I can smell it over here!
HOMELESS PERSON 4: That must of ripped a hole in his sleeping bag!
HOMELESS PERSON 5: It was me, it was me! Now shut up, will you!
HOMELESS PERSON 1: What crawled up your arse and died?
HOMELESS PERSON 5: The food at that van—it's given me crook guts.
VOICES: Shut up, go to sleep…

The voices fade out.

PETA: See what I mean? Anyway, I can't sit here all night gossiping. I'm on a mission.
SAM: Are you a—a—er… er…
PETA: Oh, I gave up being an a—a—er a long time ago.
SAM: I mean, you know—
PETA: Am I a real woman? Or a man in a dress? Is that what you're trying to ask? You're a curious little thing, aren't you? I bet you're asking yourself—is she pre-op or post?
SAM: No, no—
PETA: I bet you're dying to know. Would you like to see for yourself?

PETA makes as if to lift up her dress. SAM *turns away.*

SAM: No, no I don't want to know.
PETA: Oh, happy to accept me as you find me, are you?
SAM: Yeah…
PETA: Very well. Now, if you've got enough for your school project, I'd better be on my way.
SAM: What school project?
PETA: And make sure you spell my name right. Peta with an 'a'.
SAM: Wait on, what project?
PETA: You are just a tourist, aren't you?

SAM: What do you mean?

PETA: You and your girlfriends having a little adventure, sleeping out with the homeless people. All huddled up together all nice and cosy. Then in the morning, back to your nice warm bed in the suburbs. And then you can write it all up in one of those big scrapbooks, pictures stuck in of derroes that you've cut out of the newspaper. I hope you get good marks. But where are your friends? Didn't turn up? Or couldn't hack it?

SAM: I'm not here for a school project or anything like that.

PETA: Oh, I see—you're out here to show compassion for the homeless, are you? Is it Sleepout time again? I hope you have lots of very generous sponsors.

SAM: I don't have any sponsors!

PETA: Pity.

SAM: Look, thank you very much for helping me with Mr Sleaze just then. I'm not here because I want to be. I left home. Kicked out really. I'm sorry I've upset you somehow. I'll leave you alone, okay? I'll go.

HOMELESS MEN: Yay!

PETA: Oh, darling, I'm sorry. I'm harmless. Homeless and harmless. Just a little bit crazy, but that comes with the territory. There's a lot of us out here in the community now. Community care, they call it, and see how much the community cares? They let us sleep in their parks.

The beam of a flashlight stabs the darkness. HOMELESS MEN *wake up, moaning and groaning.*

HOMELESS MEN: Oh, shit! The ranger.

RANGER: Come on, you blokes—you can't sleep here! You've been warned. Come on, move it along.

PETA: Except when the Olympics are on! The eyes of the world are upon us! Come on, you look hungry. There's a food van up near the station. I hope you've got a strong stomach.

SCENE NINE: IN THE SUBURBS 3—DINNER TIME

PARENTS: [*off stage*] Dinner time. Come and sit down. Wash your hands first.

TEENAGER 1: Dinner time at my place ranges from about six thirty to nine thirty.

TEENAGER 2: Six thirty, dinner time, in the dining room, on the dining room table.
TEENAGER 3: Dinner is always at seven-thirty, around that.
TEENAGER 6: [*a girl*] We don't, like, have a time like six thirty to nine, it's five o'clock or there's no dinner.
TEENAGER 5: [*a boy*] God, that's so early!
TEENAGER 6: I know, 'cos, like, we used to do it when we lived overseas, and still do it.
TEENAGER 4: I'd be starving by ten!
TEENAGER 6: That's the rule: my dad watches the news and everyone else has to shut up.
TEENAGER 1: Mum usually cooks. Some days, on Tuesdays, I cook. We have a timetabley-thing, but I'm not a good cook. I can only cook—what can I cook?
TEENAGER 5: There's three of us, me and my mum and my sister. Most of the meals are cooked by me, more often than not.
TEENAGER 4: Men are the best cooks, I just want to say that.
TEENAGER 5: Thanks.
TEENAGER 2: My dad does all the cooking in my house. He's basically the mum. He retired a few years ago. And my mum kept on working, and so, yeah, he just kind of took over the household. And, like, he runs a really tight ship, you've got to give pre-warning to dinner, like I'm talking one and two days in advance—no I'm serious, because if you don't, you just get nothing.
TEENAGER 4: I cook on Sundays—whatever I can find that's easiest to make. I got a thing today, so like tomorrow I'll do, like, chicken that's already cut up and I just have to fry it and then put the sauce into it. So Sunday's my regular day, unless I have a reason for not cooking…
TEENAGER 6: My mum is the main cook. I only cook for myself.
TEENAGER 5: Never for the family?
TEENAGER 6: [*with irony*] Yeah, I'm going to cook a roast…
TEENAGER 5: That's the easiest thing to cook, actually. Just peel the potatoes, cut 'em up, pumpkin …
TEENAGER 1: It used to always be spinach lasagne—not every night, but pretty much every week, and now I don't know—I don't keep a record of what I eat for dinner.
TEENAGER 5: We have rice, spaghetti bolognaise… steak, peas and

corn sometimes, but I do the sauce thing, so it's not really steak—it's nice. And then if I really don't want to do anything, we'll have mash potato, sausages and peas and corn. Mum likes to eat meat for some reason, I don't—can't stand it, and I've got to like handle it when it's raw. If I'm not home, they get take-out. The past three nights, I finally went home this morning and it's like, Oh! The garbage was—there were two pizza boxes and Chinese stuff and I'm thinking... [*Pulls face of frustration and exasperation*] Argh!

TEENAGER 6: There's four of us. There seems to be rice with everything for some reason. I don't know why. And carrots, and—like in a little dish. Like we were still overseas. It's kinda scary.

TEENAGER 2: Sometimes my dad eats by himself—which I really hate, 'cos he's home all day by himself, and then no-one comes home for dinner, I feel sorry for him—I don't like eating alone myself.

TEENAGER 1: Mum's doing University, she's got University work, and work—work things, and friends and stuff. So we don't really have a talking-at-the-table kind of dinner.

TEENAGER 3: After the big day, you just sit down and talk. Or she does. We're told to listen. Yeah, I sit there and listen, it's mainly her and my sisters talking to each other, and I just sit there and listen in.

TEENAGER 4: I've got a humungous family—there's six kids and Mum and Dad... We don't all fit at the table, so it's like staggered out. I'm in the middle... All the older people are out with their boyfriends or girlfriends, out getting drunk or... Mum tries to make it, like, no TV, you have to sit there eat your dinner and talk about the day's events.

ALL: [*echoing previous*] Argh...

SCENE TEN: SAM 4—CARMEN

Later that same night. PETA *enters with a bag containing bread rolls and cake.* SAM *is limping.*

SAM: Ouch, ouch, ouch! Somebody stomped on my foot. Are they always so pushy at the food vans?

PETA: Darling, you'll learn: it's a dog eat dog world.

SAM: I was wondering what was on that roll. Yuck.

PETA: A free meal and she still complains. You were just made for the streets.

SAM: You should talk. You sure you got enough cakes?

PETA: Don't be cheeky, squeaky. These aren't for me. I'm making a delivery.
SAM: Where are we going?
PETA: On a little visit. Then we'd better find you somewhere safe to stay for the night.
SAM: Where do you live?
PETA: I share a squat with a friend. Very tiny—the squat that is, not my friend. A little tiny-minded perhaps. She doesn't appreciate me bringing home strays. Besides, I think you'd like to be with people your own age, wouldn't you?

>   SAM *just shrugs.* SAM *and* PETA *approach a station wagon. The car and its occupants—*CARMEN *and her baby are melded into one creation: it's as if the car itself is alive and talking, not just the person inside.*

Hello, Carmen! Hello. Hello? No-one home?
CARMEN: Shhh, shhh hello, Peta, is that you? Shhh! Please keep your voice down. I just got the little one off to sleep.
PETA: [*whispering*] I'm sorry. Here, I brought some supplies.

>   PETA *hands the bag of food into the car.*

CARMEN: Oh, thanks some bread and—and cake! Thank you.
PETA: Yes, I was thinking of you and the Bubba and I thought—let them eat cake.
CARMEN: Thanks, you're a love.
PETA: Just call me Marie Antoinette.
CARMEN: Yeah. Why?
PETA: Oh, no reason.
SAM: It's a joke. Marie Antoinette was the one who said—
CARMEN: She's with the Government, isn't she? Community Services?
SAM: No, she's not with the Government. She's a—
CARMEN: Bloody Liberal. That'd be right. That mob don't give a rat's arse about the battlers.
SAM: She was a French queen.
CARMEN: Oh, one of Peta's mates. Sorry, love. I'm sure she meant well.
PETA: That's right, her heart was in the right place. If not, finally, her head.
CARMEN: You've lost me again.
SAM: Forget it. It's history.

CARMEN: I'll be history too, if my old man doesn't get back soon.
PETA: Any day, now, Carmen, any day now.

    CARMEN's *baby starts crying.*

CARMEN: Oh, sugar, she's started again.
PETA: I'm sorry. We'll let you get her back to sleep.
CARMEN: Hang on a tick—don't go.

    CARMEN *attends to the baby.* SAM *and* PETA *talk to one side.*

SAM: Do they live in there—inside the car?
PETA: Yes, Carmen the Car Woman, as she's been nicknamed, has been living in the car for nearly a year. Her husband Col, he was gambler, lost everything they had: house, belongings, everything—except the car. So they started living in it. Then she got pregnant, and when the baby was born he took off up north to get work fruit picking to try and earn enough for a deposit on a flat. She's expecting him back any day now.
SAM: But she can't live in a car.
PETA: She can—and she does. We scammed her a local resident's parking ticket—she can park there legally for about another month. Then the council and the cops'll probably start to heavy her.
SAM: But the baby—
PETA: She's a real sweety, isn't she? It makes me feel clucky. Well almost. But Harrison's a cutie—a real darn beauty. He was conceived and born in the car, so they named him after it.
SAM: Harrison?
PETA: Harrison Ford. Use your imagination, sweetie.
SAM: But she can't live in a car with a baby.
PETA: People live where they have to, darling.
SAM: But the baby. Surely there's a refuge or something—
PETA: Yes, yes—there's support she could get. But she can't give up the car. It's the only thing in the world that she owns and she doesn't want to lose it. So she lives in it. For the moment, anyway, it's their home. Don't worry, we keep an eye out for her... Unfortunately, the fruit picking season is well and truly over.
SAM: And Col's not back? You mean... But what'll she do?
PETA: Que sera, sera.
CARMEN: What's that, love?
PETA: Nothing. Just a little bit of French.

CARMEN: You're not still on about that Marie-Ann what's-her-face, are you?
PETA: No, no. We'd best be on our way—we didn't mean to disturb you and Harrison.
CARMEN: It wasn't you that done that. We had some unwanted visitors a bit earlier. I tell ya, there's some bad 'uns out tonight. Be careful. Real hoons. Out to cause trouble. Pyromaniacs. They tried to set the car on fire.
SAM: With you and Harrison inside it?
PETA: Not much fun for them otherwise. Anybody can set alight an empty vehicle.
CARMEN: See down there—a little pile of leaves and rubbish under the back tyre? They were trying to light that. They almost had it going. They'd poured some metho on it… Must've pinched it off some poor old bastard. I hope they didn't torch him, too.
SAM: I feel sick!
CARMEN: Anyway, they got a bit of flame going, but I threw some wet nappies on it—that put the dampeners on it. Pissed them right off. They started trying to kick the windows in—so I jumped out the other side and started chucking more dirty nappies at them, real shitty ones. They took off like I dunno what. They say opposites attract, and things that are alike repel. They were repelled alright. But they were a mean-looking pair. In from the suburbs, I reckon, out to cause trouble. So be careful out tonight, okay? Be real careful.
SAM: Do you want us to call the cops?
CARMEN: Nah, I got plenty more shitty nappies. Besides, bad enough the locals ringing the cops all the time and complaining about me. You just be careful, okay?
PETA: We will be, Carmen… See you again soon.
CARMEN: And thanks for the cakes.
PETA: I'll pass that on to Marie.

The car rolls offstage. The baby starts crying again.

CARMEN: [*offstage*] Now, now, Harrison, there's a good boy…
SAM: Hey, I wonder what she would've called her baby if they'd been living in a car that wasn't a Ford?
PETA: Well, in a Holden, he'd've been William.

SAM: William?

PETA: William Holden! Oh, you're too young!

> As PETA and SAM *chat and laugh, they are being watched from the shadows by two* HOONS.

SAM: But wait on—what if Harrison had been a girl?

> *The girls laugh. The* HOONS *begin to hiss from the shadows.*

HOONS: Sssssst! Sssst!

SAM: What was that?

> PETA *grabs her hand and pulls her away.*

PETA: Quick, follow, me, quick, quick, quick…

> *The girls run off just in time to avoid being hit by a couple of flying beer cans. The* HOONS *emerge from the shadows, laughing and sneering.*

HOON 1: See that? Dykes.

HOON 2: Yeah, fucking dykes.

HOON 1: Well, come on.

HOON 2: Yeah, come on. I'm coming, I'm coming.

> *The* HOONS *run off after* PETA *and* SAM.

SCENE ELEVEN: HOMELAND 4—UNCLE'S PLACE

In a bedroom in their Uncle's flat, ALI *and* MERINDA *are sleeping.*

The sound of a car backfiring. ALI *thrashes about as if in a nightmare.* MERINDA *gets up and crosses to his bedside.*

MERINDA It's alright Ali, it's alright! It's only the traffic. Sleep, my brother, sleep. Everything's alright.

> ALI *drifts back to a more peaceful sleep.*

[*To audience*] Our mother writes to us—finally! The situation has not improved back home. Stay in Australia as long as you can, she says.

She gives us an address of an uncle who we have never met. He lets us move in to his tiny flat in a block of redbrick units near a busy road. I'd become used to the silence of the bush that surrounded the barracks, and here the noise of the traffic, night and day, makes it difficult for me to sleep. At least I don't suffer the nightmares that torture Ali more and more. [*To* ALI] It's alright, Ali, it's only traffic. Everything's alright…

> *It is now morning.* MERINDA *prepares for school and work,* ALI *rises sluggishly, without enthusiasm for the new day. He turns on the TV and slumps down in front of it.*

What will you do today, Ali?

ALI: The same as I did yesterday and the day before that: I'll wait.

MERINDA: But we have no idea when the war might end. [*No response.*] Mum wouldn't say that it is too dangerous to come home if it wasn't true.

ALI: She says that to protect us—we should be there to protect her.

MERINDA: There's nothing we can do. If you would accept that, if you would try to learn English, or get a job, instead of just sitting all day watching— [TV]

ALI: Watching our homeland being destroyed—bombed and burnt to the ground. Our people being killed.

MERINDA: We can do nothing.

ALI: Then that's all I'm doing. Leave me alone.

MERINDA: But it's not good for you to just sit and—

ALI: I'm sick of your nagging and whining.

MERINDA: Ali, please…

ALI: Shut up!

MERINDA: I'll be going straight from school to work tonight. I'm on the late shift. You and uncle will have to feed yourselves.

> ALI *doesn't reply.*

There is plenty in the fridge…

> ALI *still doesn't reply.*

See you later.

> MERINDA *leaves.* ALI *flicks the remote control at the TV.*

NEWS READER: [*voiceover*] NATO continued its air strikes against the besieged city overnight despite growing concerns about mounting civilian casualties…

A passenger train carrying up to three hundred civilian commuters, including children…

Outside the capital, Government forces clashed with Liberation Army rebels in a bloody confrontation…

The news fades out (or under) the sounds of the battle we have heard before in the earlier war zone scene. The room becomes a battle field, we are in the war zone.

Among the other images is the image of Ali and Merinda's MOTHER *being pushed around and assaulted by soldiers.*

ALI *hurls the remote control at the TV, throws himself on his bed.*

Later that night, MERINDA *enters with a boy,* TONY. TONY *waits by the entrance as* MERINDA *enters.* ALI *stirs on his bed.*

ALI: Merinda?
MERINDA: Sorry to wake you. Have you eaten yet?
ALI: I'm not hungry.
MERINDA: Uncle?
ALI: Probably at the club. Poker machines! [*Pause*] What are you doing? It's late. Who's out there with you?
MERINDA: I have no class in the morning. I'm going to the movies with a friend.
ALI: You brought someone here?
MERINDA: Yes, I've brought a friend home. We're going to see a film.
ALI: You think so, eh? If it's one of those Australian girls, I don't think you'll be going anywhere.

  ALI *sees* TONY *waiting.*

MERINDA: Ali, Tony's not a girl…
TONY: Not the last time I looked, anyway.
MERINDA: Ali, this is Tony.
TONY: Hello, Ali, nice to meet you.

  TONY *puts out his hand, but* ALI *does not take it.* ALI *directs most of the following to* MERINDA.

ALI: He speaks—
MERINDA: Our language, yes. And his English is good too.
TONY: 'How you going, mate.'

  TONY *and* MERINDA *laugh.*

MERINDA: Tony works with me at McDonalds.
TONY: Yeah, take my word for it: don't eat there unless it's an emergency—and even then think twice!
ALI: Why have you brought him here—into our home?

MERINDA: So this is your home now—good, you must be feeling better.
ALI: I'm not joking. Why have you brought him here?
MERINDA: He's taking me to the movies. [*To* TONY] I'm ready, let's go.
TONY: Listen, Ali, it's really— [alright.]
ALI: That's not our language he speaks.
MERINDA: Yes, it is—it's the same as ours.
ALI: Where are you from?
MERINDA: Ali, he's been in Australia five years…
ALI: I asked where is he from? That accent—from the North.
TONY: Originally, my people [came from—]
ALI: Your people are slaughtering our people.
MERINDA: Ali, don't say such stupid things.
ALI: We are exiled in this stupid country because your people are killing our people—my father, my family.
MERINDA: No, Ali, please, don't talk like this.
TONY: Our family came to Australia, too, because we were driven out by war.
ALI: A war that your people started.
MERINDA: Tony didn't start the war. People like us don't make wars. Governments make the wars.
ALI: How could you bring this person to this house? If you don't care about my feelings—
MERINDA: I do care about –
ALI: [*over her*] If you don't care about my feelings, think of your Uncle—you know he lost his family, his homeland, because of these people…
TONY: Merinda, I'd better go—
MERINDA: Wait, we're going together, to the movies.

    ALI *pulls his sister back.*

ALI: You're not going anywhere with scum like this.
MERINDA: Ali!
TONY: Ali, you better take it easy.
ALI: Get out of here—get out of here now!

    ALI *pushes* TONY *back toward the door.* TONY *would like to retaliate, but doesn't.*

TONY: I'll go now, Merinda. This was a mistake.

MERINDA: No, please, wait—
TONY: I'll see you at work tomorrow.
ALI: Merinda will not be returning to work.

    TONY *goes.* MERINDA *pulls away from* ALI.

MERINDA: Ali, how could you? You are not my father! You can't do this to me!
ALI: I'm glad your father is not here to be shamed by you like this.
MERINDA: My father shamed?
ALI: Yes, to see you become friends—become lovers maybe—with people who want to kill us, drive us from our own land.
MERINDA: Tony and his family came here before this war. They were driven out of their homeland by another war. Tony has nothing to do with what is happening to us.
ALI: His people—his people right now are waging war on us.
MERINDA: Tony is not waging war on us. We are in Australia now. We are not at war in Australia.
ALI: I am telling you: you will not have anything to do with his kind—is that clear?
MERINDA: And you say I shame our father? My father's soul was never as bitter and poisoned as yours. You're the one who shames our father's memory.

    ALI *hits her across the face, shocking himself as he does so.* MERINDA *does not retaliate—she picks up her things and leaves the flat, perhaps chasing after* TONY. ALI *does not attempt to stop her or follow her.* ALI *stands alone. The sound effects of the war zone fade up and out.*

END OF ACT ONE

ACT TWO

SCENE TWELVE: SAM 5—THE SQUAT

An inner city squat, a dirty, candlelit room with some crates and boxes for furniture, and dirty torn mattresses scattered over the floor. Two girls occupy the place: the younger, CHRISSIE, *is talking on a mobile phone.* LISA, *older and tougher looking, is strumming her guitar and getting fed up with* CHRISSIE's *conversation.*
PETA *and* SAM *enter—they have been running.*

PETA: Hello! Hello! Is anyone home? Lisa!
>LISA *jumps up from her bed with a cricket bat, ready to strike.*

Lisa, Lisa—it's alright, it's alright—it's only me, it's only me.
LISA: Peta! Jesus! What the—? And if it's only you, then who the hell's that?
PETA: She's fine—this is Sam.
LISA: What's up? The cops chasing you?
PETA: Some redneck hoons.
LISA: Aw great, why don't you just draw them a map to the squat, why don't you?
SAM: I think we lost them in the laneways.
PETA: They didn't see us come in here.
LISA: Just as well.
PETA: Sam, this is Lisa.
SAM: Hi.
LISA: Hi.
SAM: You live here?
LISA: What's it look like to you?
PETA: This is Lisa's squat. Be it ever so humble. You've been here a while now, haven't you? A couple of years?
LISA: I dunno. Too long. But maybe not much longer. They're starting to redevelop soon. More crappy overpriced terraces. More yuppies moving in.

PETA: Oh, dear, there goes the neighbourhood... You have a new flatmate?
LISA: That's Chrissie, my sister.
CHRISSIE: Hi.
LISA: This is Peta and Sam.
PETA: Chrissie's moved in for a while, has she?
LISA: A couple of nights maybe. If she lives that long. When I saw her she was about to get into a car with some real scumbag.
CHRISSIE: I nearly went with him. I was starting to freak out that I'd end up sleeping in a doorway. He offered me a bed at least. So, thanks for that. I was pretty out of it—I've never gone that far before. God, what a sleaze bag he was. Er! I'm getting a flashback of his big slobbering mouth and his tongue hanging out.
SAM: Hey, wow, did he have like these ugly bulging trousers and—
LISA: That was him—Mr Sleaze himself.
SAM: He tried to get me to go with him, too. Peta saved me.
CHRISSIE: Hey, you guys are cool.
PETA: We're just a couple of warrior princesses at heart.
SAM: You run away from home?
CHRISSIE: I haven't lived at home for yonks 'cos of me old man. I've been staying at different refuges, short term mostly, till I can find something more permanent. But the last place I was at, they kicked me out for a week.
SAM: Why?
CHRISSIE: Aw, stupid rules they have.
LISA: Tell them the full story.
CHRISSIE: Oh, I was rostered for cleaning duties. And, you know, I missed my turn.
SAM: And they kicked you out just for that?
CHRISSIE: Well, I abused the worker. He was a real dork anyway. He was picking on me.
LISA: He was asking you to do your rostered cleaning.
CHRISSIE: Well, I couldn't do it right then, could I? I was a making a call, you know. I was on me phone, and he started hassling me. So I told him to leave me alone.
LISA: Not exactly in those words.
CHRISSIE: I told him to go fuck himself. Okay?

PETA: And they suspended you for that. Is there no justice in the world?
CHRISSIE: Well you know—it's not as if the bathroom wasn't gonna still be dirty in a few more minutes. He was just on a power trip.
PETA: Now you're here, I wonder if that means there's no more room at the inn.
LISA: For Sam?
PETA: Just for the night. Perhaps? She'll probably head home in the morning, after a good night's sleep.
SAM: I will not be going home.
LISA: Yeah, don't be too sure. I reckon go home while you can, while you have a choice.
PETA: Listen to Lisa. She knows what she's talking about. She's been on the streets since she was twelve. She was once in a documentary about homeless kids.
LISA: Yeah, thanks Peta.
PETA: It was on the ABC. You were very good. I quite enjoyed it. They were talking about a sequel, weren't they? They never contacted you again?
LISA: Will you shut up about that, Peta?
PETA: I'm just saying I like your work.
LISA: Thanks… Anyway, I've had no choice but to survive on the streets.
SAM: I don't have a choice, either. I don't want to go home. I'm not going back to that place, never ever.
LISA: Suit yourself. There's a mattress in the corner.
PETA: Thanks Lisa, darling. I owe you a favour, you raver.
LISA: Yeah, there's one thing but—I dunno, but I've heard Billy's back up from Melbourne. I thought youse were him when you come barging in before.
PETA: I see. That's not such good news.
SAM: Er, who's Billy? Can't I stay here if Billy turns up?
LISA: If Billy turns up, none of us will be staying here.
PETA: Billy's a bit of a handful.

> BILLY *enters, maybe wearing a beanie and a hooded jacket and carrying a backpack. He is very speed-y and hyped up.*

BILLY: What's that you saying about Billy?
PETA: Oh, Billy, right on cue. Just like we were in a play or something!

LISA: Oh, shit.

BILLY: Yeah? You don't look too happy to see me?

LISA: Billy. It's cool. I've been expecting ya. I heard you were back in town. Where ya been?

BILLY: Just around. Up the Cross, catching up with people. You having a party? Who's this?

LISA: You know Peta.

BILLY: Yeah.

PETA: Nice to see you again, too, Billy.

LISA: [*indicating*] Chrissie and Sam. They're crashing here for the night.

BILLY: Any room for an old friend?

LISA: Maybe not tonight, eh, Billy? It's a bit of a full house.

BILLY: Yeah, yeah, that's cool, I don't mind a bit of a squeeze. Keep warm, eh?

LISA: Maybe not tonight Billy. You look a bit out of it.

BILLY: Yeah, I got some gear. You want a taste?

LISA: No, Billy. I've been clean for six months. And I want to stay that way. And I don't want you bringing any in here. You got any cash for a hotel?

BILLY: Hey, I got any cash or what? Check this out.

He throws his back pack at LISA, *who nearly drops it. It is very heavy.*

LISA: Jesus!

BILLY: Look.

He shakes the bag—it jingles. Laughing, he plunges his hand in and pulls out a handful of coins. He showers his companions in them.

Go on, help yourselves. There's plenty for everyone.

CHRISSIE: Really?

BILLY: Yeah, yeah, go for your life.

He throws more coins around. CHRISSIE *starts picking some up.* BILLY*'s mood changes quickly.*

Hey, don't be too greedy, you little pig.

He kicks her away.

CHRISSIE: [*almost in tears*] Hey, that hurt.

LISA: Billy, ease up, will ya?
SAM: Have you been busking?

>BILLY *laughs at her.*

BILLY: Busking, that's a good one. You can see me singing for my supper.
SAM: Well, where did you get all the—
PETA: Remember, kitten: curiosity killed the cat
BILLY: Yeah, ask no questions—I'll tell you no lies… But here's a clue. [*From his pocket* BILLY *pulls out a set of keys and dangles them in the air.*] Hey, what do you think these are?
SAM: They're keys…
BILLY: Of course, they're frigging keys, any dickwit can see that. Keys to what? That's the question.
LISA: If you're going to tell us, Billy, just tell us. No-one's in the mood for games.
BILLY: Another clue: right now I'm Telstra's worst nightmare.
SAM: They're keys to payphones?
BILLY: Yeah, cool eh? I cleaned out at least two dozen between here and Central. In, out, in, out. They don't know what hit 'em.
SAM: But where did you get the keys to payphones?
BILLY: Jesus! As if I'm gonna tell you.
PETA: She can't help herself—incorrigibly curious.
BILLY: Yeah, well, anyway, Telstra's been robbing the public for long enough, eh? Why not.
PETA: He's Robin Hood at heart.
BILLY: And that's not all I got.

>BILLY *pulls a pistol out of his coat pocket.*

LISA: Jesus, Billy, what are you doing?
BILLY: Eh? What do you think? Four hundred bucks, man, that's a bargain. These things cost over fifteen hundred.
LISA: Where'd you get it?
BILLY: Up the Cross. You can get anything you want at the Cross.
LISA: Jesus, Billy what do you want a frigging gun for? Put it away, will ya?
BILLY: Chill out, will ya? You think I'm gonna shoot ya? [*He waves the gun at her*] Bang, bang—eh!

>BILLY *laughs and then realises that no-one is sharing his joke—in fact, they're all shit scared.*

LISA: Put that thing away. Go find somewhere else to crash.
BILLY: I wanna stay here with friends.
LISA: Not tonight, okay, Billy?
BILLY: Don't fucking tell me what to do, okay?
LISA: I just asked you nicely to put that thing away. Just chill out.
BILLY: Don't tell me to chill out—you chill out!
PETA: Listen, Lisa, thanks for the offer—but we'll be on our way. Goodnight.

> SAM *gets up to leave but* BILLY *points the gun at her.* SAM *freezes.*

BILLY: You scared of me?
SAM: I'm scared of guns. Please don't point it at me.
PETA: Billy, please put the gun down.
LISA: Billy—
BILLY: Shut up, will yas! Shut up!

> *A tense silence. The gun is still pointed at* SAM.

PETA: Billy, please, put it down. We're going to go now, okay? Chrissie, would you like to—
CHRISSIE: I'm staying with Lisa.
BILLY: It mightn't be loaded, you know? Mightn't be any bullets in it. What do you reckon?
PETA: I don't reckon anything, Billy. Good night, Chrissie. Lisa.

> PETA *shepherds* SAM *out.*

SAM: See yas. [*To* CHRISSIE] I'll call ya.
BILLY: Hey, take some money—you might need it—take some money.

> PETA *and* SAM *exit.* BILLY *throws a handful of coins after them.*

LISA: Billy, cut it out will ya!

> BILLY *swings the gun around and points it at* LISA.

BILLY: Shut up, I told you!

> BILLY *pulls the trigger. The pistol clicks—it is empty.* BILLY *laughs hysterically.*

SCENE THIRTEEN: IN THE SUBURBS 4—HOMELESS PEOPLE

TEENAGER 1: I was in the city for an excursion and we went to Hungry Jacks for lunch. There was this old man, y'know? Really scruffy hair-type looking person and, like, homeless—not very clean looking. And this old guy was asking people for money and he went up to my teacher and asked for some money for a bus ticket, and she goes—

TEACHER: I'm not going to give you the money, but I will buy you lunch, if that's what you want.

TEENAGER 1: And, basically, he refused the lunch and he wanted the money. And she told him, you know …

TEACHER: Where's your concession card? If you've got a senior citizen's card, you can get bus rides for free!

TEENAGER 1: And stuff like that. And, anyway, she felt better, because instead of offering him money, she offered him food because—you know, she wouldn't feel bad about not giving him any money. But anyway, it ended up he had to be chucked out, because people were sitting down and he was asking them stuff while they were eating.

TEENAGER 2: Badgering the customers?

TEENAGER 1: That's it. Badgering. And I watched it. I was really scared because I don't really like being approached by people asking for money, because I'm the kind of person who'll go, 'Yeah, this is all I've got, take it'.

TEENAGER 2: I say, 'Sorry, I don't have any spare change.' Because they say:

HOMELESS PERSON: 'Spare change?'

TEENAGER 2: It's like, I have change, but not spare change to share with you.

TEENAGER 3: Well, I was in Kings Cross, going to get my tongue pierced for the second time, and I was just, like, walking along to get to Oxford Street, and this lady—I don't know if she was homeless or not, but from the looks of her, she was not in the… not in a… proper living area. Anyway, she comes up to us and she just goes—she was like, all in tears and crying, and she could barely talk—and she goes:

LADY: Oh, can I have a dollar for a phone call and I'll give you my wedding ring?

TEENAGER 3: And it was like a real wedding ring, diamonds and all, and so I just said to her, 'Keep the wedding ring, here's the dollar anyway... Are you sure you don't need anything else?'

TEENAGER 2: How old did she look?

TEENAGER 3: Oh, about twenty-five to thirty—she wasn't that old.

TEENAGER 2: But she looked homeless... ?

TEENAGER 3: Oh, I don't know—but her hair was just matted and really disgusting. Her clothes were a bit, like, dirty, with the stains and all that, but... I'm not sure. I know I own clothes with stains on them and I walk around the street, so... She could have been in the same situation—couldn't have been bothered washing them.

TEENAGER 2: She might have been having a really bad hair day.

TEENAGER 5: Sometimes when I come home from school, there's this crazy lady who gets on the bus, and she wears shabby clothes and stuff, but she always appears to be drunk. And whenever she gets on, she, like, sits up the front—and, you know how there's the old people at the front of the bus? She just looks at them and starts swearing at them, just like—full-on, discriminating against every single person on the bus. And the whole bus just fights with this lady until she gets off... Most of the times the bus driver makes her get off the bus—because she's just like so bad... She's fully yelling at everyone, and it's just really sad.

TEENAGER 4: Well, we were down at Bondi Beach and we were all going for the bus, and there was a homeless guy standing on the corner. We ran and got on the bus, and there was another guy standing on the steps of the bus. And the bus driver says:

BUS DRIVER: Quick! Get on! Get on! Get on!

TEENAGER 4: Because he didn't want the homeless guy to get on the bus. And the homeless guy got there, and the driver went:

BUS DRIVER: Look, mate, I've told you once, I've told you twice, I don't want you on my bus.

TEENAGER 4: So he told him to go away, and then the... then the homeless guy stuck his finger up at the bus driver.

TEENAGER 2: It's not their fault they're homeless... Well, it might be their fault that they're homeless, but... I don't think it's fair to not let them on the bus. Because, hey, if you had a broken leg, and we're scruffed up you may look homeless, but you may be one of the richest men in the world. And they might think you're homeless, and they won't let you on.

TEENAGER 1: I mean, sometimes they can choose to be on the street. I've heard stories—from an officer at the Salvation Army, because we went on an excursion there for school—I've heard a story where a man—he's been homeless for about seven years or something—and he has about one point seven million dollars sitting in the bank. And, so… I don't know… he just chose to be… It's like a lifestyle choice …

TEENAGER 2: I don't know. Maybe they're just sick of, like, high society, or something like that.

SCENE FOURTEEN: SAM 6—ASSAULT

Outside in the street after leaving the squat. PETA *gives* SAM *a hug.*

PETA: Are you alright, sweetie?

> SAM *begins to sob on* PETA*'s shoulder.*

[*Singing*] You picked a bad time to leave home Lucille…

SAM: No, don't…

PETA: Well, you could have picked a better night to run away. Look, if you want to go home, I'll wait with you at the station. The trains should start running again soon.

SAM: No.

PETA: You'd prefer to be on the streets with sleaze bags, drunken hoons and gun-toting psychopaths than take your chances with CityRail? Hmm, I can see where you're coming from… I guess we'll have to go back to my humble abode after all, and when I say humble, I'm not exaggerating. And there we will await the rosy-fingered dawn, as they say in the classics. Rosy-fingered dawn? Sounds a bit rude, doesn't it? I mean I hope Dawn didn't mind being…

> *A beer can narrowly misses them.* PETA *and* SAM *freeze,* PETA *protectively holding* SAM.

Oh, shit.

> *The two* HOONS *step out of the shadows and approach the girls.*

HOON 1: Fucking dykes. We'll teach you.

HOON 2: Yeah, we'll teach you.

The HOONS *attack* PETA *and* SAM, *going particularly for* PETA, *kicking and punching her.* SAM *somehow manages to slip away and starts dialling out on her mobile phone.*

SAM: [*into phone*] Hello, police, police, help us, please…

The HOONS *kick* PETA *to the ground. They turn and look at* SAM *and move towards her. A police siren sounds.*

SCENE FIFTEEN: HOMELAND 5—RETURN HOME

A POLITICIAN *is surrounded by* REFUGEES *at the barracks.*

POLITICIAN: You are deemed to be no longer in need of protection and, apart from those too sick to travel, you are to be sent back home.

REFUGEES *react to news.*

It is not that we are without compassion for you people. We are not heartless, but please, be reasonable: it is now time for you to return home. We are satisfied that you have no claims that would single you out for persecution when you return home.

MOTHER: Don't come home yet, it is still too dangerous.

MERINDA *and* ALI *in their flat.*

MERINDA: We can't go.

ALI: Have you no concern at all for your own mother? Don't you want to see her? Don't you think she wants to see her daughter?

MERINDA: I love my mother! She is the one who says it is still unsafe to return. Perhaps if we bring her to Australia now that it's safe for her to travel…

ALI: She won't come to Australia. Everything she has, everything and everyone she knows is back there, in our homeland.

MERINDA: Except her children.

ALI: That's why we must return.

MERINDA: I don't want to go home—I am scared.

ALI: I will look after you.

MERINDA: I don't want to go back.

ALI: For your mother's sake, you will do as you are told!

MERINDA: If you go back, you may very well be sent to prison. You were supposed to fight in their army.

ALI: And if you stay here, you will end up in prison too.

POLITICIAN: By law, those that do not return will become illegal migrants and the department will be required to take them into detention. The barracks will become a short-term detention centre, until arrangements can be made to hold the detainees in larger centres.

The POLITICIAN *exits. The* REFUGEES *are marshalled off. They form queues with their suitcases similar to images we have seen earlier.* MERINDA *and* ALI *are nearly finished packing their own bags.*

MERINDA: Ali, I'm not going.

ALI: I am taking you home whether you like it or not, do you understand that?

MERINDA: But this is my home now—Australia.

ALI: Your home is where you grew up. Where your family is, where you belong.

MERINDA: I could belong in Australia, if only people would let me. I have made friends here. I speak the language. I feel safe here.

ALI: But it is not your home.

MERINDA: But it could be. Who says I can only have one home?

ALI: You will feel differently when we leave.

MERINDA: No, no you might feel differently when we leave. You will be glad to get away from here—you hate it here. But I'm not you. Why can't you understand how I feel? Why can't you see what's in my heart?

ALI: There is no time for this.

MERINDA: Listen to me, Ali. I will never forget our homeland. If I can escape the bloodshed and the misery of a place I can no longer bear to live in, why do you try and stop me?

ALI: Because you have a duty to return. I have a duty to take you back.

MERINDA: Duty! You're as bad as any of the soldiers who terrorised us at home.

ALI: Shut up—how dare you speak to me like this!

MERINDA: That's why you want to go home—so that you can get your revenge on the people who hurt us. And the whole cycle of hatred and war and revenge and killing goes on and on. I don't want any more of that. I'm not going back to it.

ALI: Shut up! Shut up! It's not true what you say.

MERINDA: It is. I saw the way you looked at Tony that day. Your eyes were filled with hatred. It frightens me.

ALI: So it is that bastard Tony who is behind all this.

MERINDA: It is nothing to do with him.

There is the sound of a car horn blaring outside.

ALI: Come on, our Uncle is waiting. Get your things—we're going.

ALI *starts to push* MERINDA *toward her bag.* MERINDA *pushes back—they end up grappling with each other.*

MERINDA: You promised you wouldn't—

MERINDA *manages to grab the key from around* ALI's *neck, and breaks away from him.*

ALI: Give that back to me!

MERINDA: This is your key, eh? Your lucky charm, your hope for the future. Your key to go home.

ALI: Give it back. Now.

MERINDA: I could throw it out the window, into the traffic. Maybe you'd find it, maybe not.

ALI: Don't be stupid.

MERINDA: You lose this key, you can always get another one cut. If you throw my hopes for the future away, what can I do, how can I get them back?

ALI: You are talking rubbish—give me the key.

TONY *enters.*

TONY: Hello…! Hello… Hey! [*He sees* MERINDA *and* ALI] Sorry—but I heard the shouting. What's wrong?

ALI: You put her up to this.

TONY: I heard the news—I came to say goodbye.

ALI: You lying bastard! You've come to help her escape. I know what's going on now. I should fucking kill you!

ALI *picks up a kitchen knife.*

MERINDA: Ali! Don't you dare!

TONY I don't know what you're talking about.

ALI: Liar! Get out of here before I—

ALI *moves toward* TONY, *pointing the knife.*

MERINDA: Here you want your key—take it!

MERINDA *throws the key at* ALI *and steps between the two young men.*

And if you want to stab someone, stab me. They won't send me back if I'm bleeding to death.

ALI *is confused and angry, but finally drops the knife and picks up the key.*

TONY: What's going on?
MERINDA: Ali thinks you have come to help me hide here in Australia.
TONY: I don't understand.
ALI: Shut up. Just leave us. Get out.
MERINDA: I don't want to go back. I want to stay in Australia.
TONY: But, Merinda, you can't. You'll have to go back with the others.
MERINDA: Maybe you could help me to hide somewhere.
TONY: Impossible! The Government would find you. They'd deport you. They mightn't let you come back again ever.
MERINDA: Come back? I go now, how could I come back? I have no money.
TONY: I could help you. I have plans. To study, to work, to make money. I'll help you to come back. My family could sponsor you.
ALI: His family? Merinda…
TONY: But now you must do as your brother says. You must go back, for now.
ALI: Listen to him then, if you won't listen to your own brother.
MERINDA: You'd really help me to come back? Why?
TONY: You know why, Merinda, I like you. I like you very much. I would like you to come back and be with me.
ALI: Oh, my God, I'm going to be sick.

ALI *gathers up their bags. A car horn sounds outside.*

Come on, our uncle is getting impatient. We can't miss the plane. If you're coming—

ALI *gently pulls* MERINDA *away from* TONY. MERINDA *resists as he tries to pull her to the door.*

MERINDA: I'll come with you, Ali, but you must promise.
ALI: Promise what?
MERINDA: Promise you won't stop me returning to Australia.

ALI: I will take you back to my mother as I promised her. Then you can do whatever you damn well like.
MERINDA: You mean that?
ALI: Yes—I promise. I promise! What language do you want to hear it in. I promise!

> MERINDA *hugs him and takes her bag from him. The car horn sounds again.* TONY *puts out his hand to* ALI *again. This time* ALI *takes it, and they shake.*

And thank you.
TONY: Goodbye. Look after Merinda.
ALI: Ah, don't you start!

SCENE SIXTEEN: IN THE SUBURBS 5—LEAVING HOME

TEENAGER 4: I left when I was little—but I was like really little and although I'd left, I still kept the rules of parents, like not to cross the road without them. So I walked around the block and then—I came back home. But now I want to leave as soon as I possibly can. I hate living at home.
TEENAGER 3: You hate it? Even with your little room up in the roof?
TEENAGER 4: I love my room, I'll take my room with me… I'm hoping I can leave at the end of year twelve, but I don't know if that's possible. Most likely I could move in with my pop, I'm close with my pop. But my family just shits me really badly. I can say that word, can't I?
TEENAGER 3: What, 'family'?
TEENAGER 4: There's six kids, so it's a very big family. And there's like… Mum and Dad and there's heaps to be done and my mum kind of puts the emphasis on the fact that I'm a female, and I should be doing housework and stuff while the boys are out yuffaduffduff. And the boys can go somewhere, but if I wanted to go, I'd have to have a phone with me, and they'd have to know where I'm going.
PARENTS: Are they going to do drugs there? Is there alcohol there? Blah blah blah blah blah…
TEENAGER 4: And it's like, if the boys are going out, it's like:
PARENTS: Yeah, have fun. Do you want some money?

TEENAGER 4: So, I kind of rebel against that in my family. There's an older sister but she's a little suck and she gets away with everything. So, yeah, I'm trying to coach my parents.

OTHERS: Sit, Mum! Sit! Roll over! Give me money!

TEENAGER 5: The way my life's going now, I feel that I'm going to be on the streets by the end of two months... When I was at home it was a lot easier, but now... what I'm going through now is a lot harder than when I was living at home. When I was living at home, I wanted to get out and I wanted to be my own person, be, y'know, independent... But now I've been out of home five years, and it's just like, I'm out of here, all alone. If I did get kicked out of my place, where I'm living now, I'd probably go to my mum, but I probably couldn't live there, because I've lived out of home for so long. Going back with my mum and my brother, I'd probably feel strange about doing it...

TEENAGER 6: Well, I've been wanting to move out since forever, and when I finished high school I'd be ready to move out, but I just didn't have any money. And, as it is, I'm still dependent on my parents... But I actually really, really want to live on my own and do it all myself. But I know that I won't be able to handle it. I'd like to think I'd be able to handle it, but I know I wouldn't be able to, like financially, having to be on my own, and having to do everything myself, like having to cook my own meals all the time. Because usually it's like, Oh... y'know, Dad's going to be making dinner, so I don't have to worry about that. The fact that I take everything for granted—that there'll be hot water for ever, ever and ever, and that I'll have somebody that can drive me everywhere. Well, I don't particularly want to have a cold shower, because I don't like cold showers. And I hate catching public transport.

I could quit my course, and get a job straight away, which is kind of scary in itself, because that means I'd actually have to get a job, and I think that would make me more independent, which is probably what I'm scared of, actually, being independent, even though I'd like to be independent.

TEENAGER 3: I can see myself having my nice little apartment with my new kitchen and the ocean view and all that... I'd like to leave as soon as possible. Just finish school and stuff. My dad lives with his girlfriend, and I know that if worst came to worst I could always live with him, even though, like, his girlfriend's, y'know, upper class and stuff like that…

I think very much I've always been dependent on myself. Like, when you were saying about public transport, and that—like, my mum doesn't drive me round much, and, like, I've been washing my own clothes since I was in year three… And like, y'know, my mum cooks dinner probably twice a week, and on the other nights we just have whatever there is and, like, I just work and I usually just pay for stuff myself. I've got a part-time job… I'm a checkout chick at Coles. And, yeah, it's good, because as you get older you can spend a lot more… and, yeah, I'd like to leave at the end of year twelve… My older sister left home for a year, and then she came back and she was really grateful that she had somewhere to go, because when she went up to Queensland to live, like, it was hard for her, like, with money and everything.

TEENAGER 1: I think I will end up missing my parents, even though I'd like to get away from them… [*Pause*] All those awkward silences. I'd like to get some place with friends. I suppose I just want to get out as soon as possible. Except, I don't have the money for it.

TEENAGER 4: I'm going to win the lottery!

TEENAGER 1: I sell Lotto. I could sell you the winning ticket.

TEENAGER 4: Alright, cool! Me and Jackie are going to get a house together!

TEENAGER 1: Yep! We're going to party together—you're all invited.

ALL: Yay!

They all exit in party mode.

SCENE SEVENTEEN: SAM 7—PHONE HOME / HOMELAND 6—NO HOME

Simultaneous images:

SAM *is sitting alone in what might be a waiting room of a hospital or a police station.*

ALI *and* MERINDA *carry their bags to a pile of rubble of what once was their home; they stand there looking at it.*

SAM *pulls out her mobile phone and makes a call. In another area of the performing space,* JO *answers her phone.*

JO: Hello?

SAM: Hi Jo.

JO: Sam? Sam! Where are you? How are you? Mum's gone berserk. She said the police rang. She said you were nearly killed and raped and arrested. She's gone to the police station to get you. How are you? Are you alright? Mum said—

SAM: Hey, Jojo—just calm down. I'm alright, I'm alright. I just had a rough night, okay? A friend got bashed up. They think she'll be alright.

JO: Are you coming home?

SAM: They're sending me home, but I don't think I'll be staying.

JO: Aw, Sam…

SAM: I don't want to live somewhere because I'm too scared not to be there. I want to be at home because it's somewhere I want to be.

JO: Maybe things with Mum'll get better…

SAM: Maybe. Not yet. I'm sorry, Jo.

    JO *hangs up the phone.*

MERINDA: When we arrive back home, we find that our mother is alive and well, but living with some family friends some streets away from our old house, at least where our old house used to stand.

    Standing over the debris that was once his old house, ALI *takes the key from around his neck and holds it in his fist for a moment, and then throws it in the rubble.* MERINDA *puts a comforting arm around her brother. They then pick up their bags and move off.*

DOM: So what is it about humans and homes? If you're not running away from it, or you're trying to get back to it, you're destroying it! Sheeesh—I don't know, compared to you, I think I was better off under the front doorstep waiting for my slice of bread. Ah, well each to their own… [*He picks up* ALI's *keys*] Well, what are you waiting for? If you're lucky enough to have one, go home!

THE END

The Yum Yum Room
Stephen House

STEPHEN HOUSE has had sixteen plays and four short films produced, and four solo exhibitions. He has won two AWGIE awards from the Australian Writers' Guild, an Adelaide Fringe Award, and was shortlisted for the Patrick White and Queensland Premier's Drama Awards. He has received international residencies from the Australia Council to Canada, USA and Ireland, an Asia-link literature residency to India and an Island of Residencies to Tasmania. He has performed in productions of his work both nationally and internationally.

Stephen House as Dad, Justine Henschke as Annabelle, and Jamie Harding as Tom in the 2009 Come Out 2009 Professional Collective production. (Photo: Francesco Photography)

The Yum Yum Room was first produced by Professional Collective at Wehl Street Theatre, Mount Gambier, on 14 May 2008, with the following cast:

TOM	Alec Ackland
ANNABELLE	Rachel Bronca
MRS MAC	Karen Colemen
DAD	Stephen House

Director, Stephen House
Lighting, Monica Hart
Original Sound, Neumeria

The Yum Yum Room was commissioned by The City of Mount Gambier.

CHARACTERS

TOM, around 17
DAD, around 45
ANNABELLE, around 17
MRS MAC, 75–80

SETTING

The play is set in Mount Gambier in the South East of Australia. The minimalist set needs to serve a range of places / spaces including: a small shed on a remote piece of land; the living room and kitchen of Dad and Tom's house; and Mrs Mac's front porch. There is an unnamed vacant downstage space where other action occurs.

SCENE ONE

TOM *stands alone in the shed.* DAD *stands alone in the living room.*

TOM: It is a place that has always been mine.
DAD: His place.
TOM: No-one else's in the whole world.
DAD: I just let him go… I have to now, almost completely. I did then too, I suppose, in a kind of way.
TOM: I remember when it began.
DAD: Our way… him and me… here.
TOM: This place and me, coming here.
DAD: He has always wandered off alone.
TOM: I was six… nearly seven; and it was not too long after she went away… I think.
DAD: He needed too be alone then… still does… but then so do I sometimes.
TOM: Finding this place; in a paddock behind the church.
DAD: Just let him go.
TOM: By myself.
DAD: I can understand it.
TOM: What's best… still is I think.
DAD: A son grows into a man… nearly a man, and confronts every bloody thing a father says… probably what a mother would say… would've said… if she was here.

> TOM *looks at* DAD *and moves into the kitchen.*

I can make my own decisions thank you very much!
DAD: [*to* TOM] I know! I know! But we're sharing a house… sharing a life; somehow.
TOM: You drive me so bloody crazy sometimes Dad!
DAD: A view of the world that is definitely not the same.
TOM: Pick, pick, pick… all the time.
DAD: I worry… that's all it is.
TOM: Well it's my business… Okay!
DAD: Okay!

DAD *wipes down the table, cleans the dishes etc.* TOM *moves away a little.*

[*Whispering, to the audience*] He has a hole in the heart.
TOM: [*calling*] And you have a hole in the head.
DAD: Don't be so bloody rude Tom.
TOM: Don't you.
DAD: And he just doesn't take the care... I wish he would.
TOM: You! Not me! You!
DAD: You should.
TOM: You should shut up sometimes.
DAD: Tom.
TOM: Like I said... it's my body... so would you please mind your business, for once.
DAD: Okay, okay... I know.
TOM: Do you?
DAD: Yes... I do! [*Whispering*] And Asthma. He has asthma too.

He calls to TOM *as he moves out of the kitchen.*

Tom have you got your puffer?
TOM: Yes!
DAD: Did you take your tablet?
TOM: Yes!

Tom moves to the shed.

I walk away from him more now, alone.
DAD: I can relate to it.
TOM: Together, but alone; that's our way.
DAD: There is an old shed behind the church.
TOM: [*in the shed*] Quiet and unused; no-one around; silent; he doesn't come here... never has. I told him not to.
DAD: I respect his privacy.
TOM: My time.
DAD: It's only five minutes away.
TOM: My place.
DAD: I knew where he was; when he was little I mean. I even knew when he found that place at six or seven years old, and made it his own. I'd watch him go, sneak off to there, follow him and listen to him to know he was safe.

TOM: I had my secrets; my control over what is now... what was and what will be.

DAD: There is an old lady... Mrs Mac who lives next to the church; has since he was a little boy.

A dim light comes up on MRS MAC, *slowly rocking back and forth in a rocking chair.*

TOM: She was the only person who knew my special place, apart from Dad; I didn't really mind her knowing; she'd leave me alone... like Dad would too I suppose.

MRS MAC: Hello little Tommy boy... hello.

She waves her stick and laughs.

[*Calling to* DAD] I know when he is in there; I see everything sitting around here all day by myself; and I'll keep my eye on him.

DAD: [*calling to* MRS MAC] Well I really appreciate that. He's only six.

MRS MAC: Not a problem fella... not a problem at all.

DAD: He has a bit of a health problem, problems, and I worry; a hole in the heart.

MRS MAC: The little boy is okay, I'm sure.

DAD: And asthma too.

MRS MAC: I can see him come and go from here. He looks well enough to me.

Lights dim on MRS MAC *as she laughs, rocking back and forth.*

The Yum Yum Room.

DAD: None of this has been easy, alone with him. I wish it had been, was now... but it hasn't, and still isn't.

TOM: My dad has had times he has not been that happy.

DAD: I'm better now... I think. I am, Tom.

TOM: And he goes on and on at me! Him! My funny, strange, crazy, weird dad.

DAD: I just go through day to day; do the best I can. Just bumbling along.

TOM: Bloody Dad.

He smiles.

DAD: Bloody Tom.

He smiles.

TOM: He's a bit lost sometimes.
DAD: Only sometimes! I'm human, Tom. Being me hasn't been all that easy.
TOM: Me too! This and us; that… back then.
DAD: Back then.
TOM: Shit!
DAD: How could you do it to him, I said to her… choose some bloody loser over your own son; a green station wagon in a cloud of dust.
TOM: Just like that.
DAD: I mean, of course it was over between us—had been for years—us, me and the way I am; but how could you do it to him… our little Tom? We watched you drive away.
TOM: My mum; in some stranger's green car.
DAD: Well I'm not drinking so much now, and I'm going to stay this way this time. I am!
TOM: He has always cared for me.
DAD: It's the drink… the bloody drink that gets to me; that I stay away from now.
TOM: But he goes on and on about my health, about asthma and the bloody hole in my heart.
DAD: I do! I go on and on and on; I can hear myself sometimes.
TOM: The hole in my life.
DAD: [*calling to him*] Now just you wait a minute, my boy. You are no different to anyone else mate.
TOM: [*calling back*] Then why do you go on and on… about everything! It really pisses me off.
DAD: I still see that little boy… that's why. And I want to care for you… everyday.

> *Light children's music plays. Flashback to* TOM *as a young boy.* TOM *and* DAD *move into the vacant space and face each other.*

TOM: Daddy?
DAD: Yes my little boy… my little mate?
TOM: Why can't we have my friends here, at our place, to sleep over? Why do I go to their places and they don't come here… ever?
DAD: Because some of the mummies only like it when there is another mummy there; not just a dad, mate, not just a dad.
TOM: Why?

DAD: I don't know.
TOM: Where is my mummy?
DAD: I don't know, mate… I don't know.

They turn away from each other. TOM *goes back to the shed.* DAD *goes back to the house.*

How do you tell a little kid anything that's real and hard and painful and cruel; how?
TOM: Why? Is it because my dad was drinking for awhile?
DAD: A day at a time.
TOM: He's not now.
DAD: How do you say to the world, that I just do it a day at a time?
TOM: He plays with me, and takes me to school; and me and dad laugh and joke lots; and he cooks me special dinners and takes me swimming in the lake when it's hot.
DAD: How do you say that it is my little mate… just like it is?
TOM: A second-hand bike instead of a shiny new one.
DAD: One day you will have everything… everything you want, everything you never had.
TOM: When will my mum come back here?
DAD: I don't know mate.
TOM: It's okay, Dad.
DAD: Is it?
TOM: Yeah… I suppose.
DAD: Over and over he would say it to me after she went away;
TOM: I love you Daddy; I love you Daddy…
DAD: And sometimes in the middle of the night he would pad into my room like a little monkey and climb into my bed; and I knew it was because he didn't want to wake up and find me leaving… like he did her; a green station wagon and a cloud of dust.
TOM: I do love you, Dad.

Silence.

And I found my other place for me.
DAD: So if he has this place he goes to; fixed up by him, for him, and then let him have it.
TOM: My secret.
DAD: It's his secret, his special place… for him… for Tom.

TOM: The Yum Yum Room.
DAD: The bloody Yum Yum Room.
> *He laughs.*

TOM: That's what I call it.
> *Lights come up slowly on* MRS MAC *in her rocking chair.*

MRS MAC: The Yum Yum Room.
> *She laughs and rocks.*

TOM: [*as a little boy*] I'm only six and this is my fort to protect me for ever and ever.
DAD: Well that's a good thing I said to her, Mrs Mac, good that he talks to you.
MRS MAC: Sometimes he comes in for a glass of cordial and a biscuit. He's a lovely little boy; and I think you do a wonderful job with him.
DAD: Really?
MRS MAC: Yes… you do.
DAD: You really think that?
TOM: [*calling to* DAD] I'm friends with an old lady called Mrs Mac, Daddy.
DAD: Well that's a surprise! I never knew that, my little mate.
TOM: She's my special friend.
DAD: [*to* MRS MAC] You just tell me if he bothers you.
MRS MAC: No, no! How could a little boy like him ever bother me? I never had kids and so no grandkids either.
TOM: And Mrs Mac stays away from my Yum Yum Room.
MRS MAC: I'm not going in there bothering him; it's his place. Everyone needs a bit time to themselves.
DAD: Do you think?
MRS MAC: Of course they do.
DAD: Even a kid?
MRS MAC: Yes! Why not? Even an old, old lady like me.
TOM: A castle perched on a rocky cliff.
MRS MAC: High up in the icy wind.
TOM: A spaceship circling the world round and round.
MRS MAC: Amongst the shining silver stars.
TOM: A boat travelling far and wide over the high seas.

MRS MAC: The Yum Yum Room.

She cackles away.

DAD: Sometimes I would quietly go there and listen to him from out the back.
TOM: Pirates! There are bloody pirates invading my boat.
DAD: Just to make sure he was okay.
MRS MAC: He's just fine, Dad.
DAD: In there alone, babbling on in a world he's created. Maybe it's better than the one I gave him.
MRS MAC: It's all just fine.
DAD: Really?
MRS MAC: You've done the best you could.
DAD: Haven't you heard the stories about me?
MRS MAC: Stories are stories. You have done alright, Dad. I see lots. Lots and lots! An old woman sitting around and wandering around town alone does.

Lights fade out on DAD *and* MRS MAC.

TOM: [*present day*] The Yum Yum Room… still now… seventeen years old… me.

Hip-hop music plays.

And that's what I still call it now too. But now…now! It's a cool bar on a New York street; a hip-hop club where I am king; a gangster den in a city shadowed by buildings a hundred stories high; my studio to create music. It is sometimes a place where I come and get stoned. [*He stimulates smoking a bong.*] Sometimes; and perform my songs. [*He dances.*] It's a plush hotel room where I take my special girls. [*He stops dancing and moves his hands seductively over himself.*] Those girls who are on the cover of magazines. [*The music is turned up and he dances.*] Pimp it up man!

Lights come up low on ANNABELLE, *downstage.*

Those beautiful, sexy girls who hold my arm and go with me to parties, nightclubs and premieres of my movies and they love me and want me, and I love them too; and I'm famous and wonderful and everything I thought I could ever be; and they come here, the hot girls, to my very cool flat in a big bloody highrise overlooking the sea and we make love I suppose; well I suppose we would, wouldn't we? Have sex… me and them; me and her… and we do; yep we certainly bloody do… I wish!

Lights go down in the shed and the music fades out.

SCENE TWO

TOM *approaches* ANNABELLE.

TOM: Thank you for that back there… before, but you know— you don't have to—
ANNABELLE: I know.
TOM: You didn't have to… I can—look after—
ANNABELLE: They are just total idiots; that's what it is.
TOM: Yeah, I know.
ANNABELLE: Total!
TOM: But you don't have to save me from their crap.
ANNABELLE: I know!
TOM: I can look after myself.
ANNABELLE: Why did they say all that to you?
TOM: Because they are bloody idiots… that's why!
ANNABELLE: I know.
TOM: I just tell them to piss off.
ANNABELLE: Me too. I haven't been in town long.
TOM: I know; I haven't seen you… much.
ANNABELLE: Much?
TOM: Well not too much; I mean… I have seen you though.
ANNABELLE: I know.
TOM: You know what?
ANNABELLE: Well I know you've seen me, because I saw you watching me the other day, when I got on the bus.
TOM: No I wasn't!
ANNABELLE: Okay! You weren't then.
TOM: Actually I was.
ANNABELLE: I know you were.

They laugh. MRS MAC *wanders past, leaning on her stick.*

MRS MAC: Hi Tom.
TOM: Hello Mrs Mac.

ANNABELLE: Hello.

MRS MAC: Hello there dear. Aren't you pretty as ever? Isn't she pretty as can be Tom?

TOM: Yeah.

MRS MAC: I'm Mrs Mac. That's what everyone calls me.

ANNABELLE: I'm Annabelle.

MRS MAC: Annabelle. Well I better get going then.

> MRS MAC *wanders off, cackling to herself as she exits.*

A young fella and young girl as pretty and young and happy as can be.

TOM: She lives near us.

ANNABELLE: Okay.

TOM: I've known her since I was a little boy.

ANNABELLE: Really?

TOM: Yeah.

ANNABELLE: Why were those kids saying all that stuff to you back there?

TOM: I don't know.

ANNABELLE: Well why did they call you that then?

TOM: I don't know… Okay!

ANNABELLE: Okay!

TOM: They call me a million names. You didn't have to come and bloody save me; you know that. I can look after myself.

ANNABELLE: I actually didn't come over there just for you! I wanted to tell them what I thought, that's all.

TOM: Why have you come here to this stupid town anyway?

ANNABELLE: My mum has a got a job here as a nurse; and I was going to stay in Melbourne with my dad and then he got a job in Sydney and I decided to come here with Mum and do year twelve.

TOM: It's good that you had the option to go with either of them.

ANNABELLE: I know. Who do you live with?

TOM: My dad; just out of town.

ANNABELLE: Where's your Mum?

TOM: I don't know.

ANNABELLE: Oh… sorry.

TOM: That's okay… I never have known her really. I hardly even remember her.

ANNABELLE: Oh.

TOM: Yeah. He's an artist, my dad.

ANNABELLE: That's cool.

TOM: Yeah.

ANNABELLE: I haven't seen you at school much… I have once I think.

TOM: That's because I hardly ever go, and I'm leaving school anyway… I hate it… and one day soon I'll leave here too… this stupid town.

ANNABELLE: I hope not too soon.

TOM: Why?

ANNABELLE: Why?

TOM: Yes, why?

ANNABELLE: Because I like you… that's why.

TOM: Okay.

ANNABELLE: Yeah… okay.

TOM: Cool.

ANNABELLE: What will you do… if you leave school?

TOM: I've already got a part-time job at McDonald's. I'll just do more hours and then… do my music probably.

ANNABELLE: Your music?

TOM: Yeah, I want to make my own hip-hop music; if I can save up for the cd mixers. I want to get two eventually, and one day be a DJ in some city somewhere… maybe Melbourne first and then… mmm… maybe New York or LA.

ANNABELLE: Cool! That's really cool. I absolutely love hip-hop!

TOM: Really?

ANNABELLE: Yep. I like the Aussie hip-hop most.

TOM: Well that's what mine will be. You want to hear some of my music sometime?

ANNABELLE: Yeah… I'd love to. You are an artist too… like your dad.

TOM: Well I suppose I am… but not like my dad… Like I am… my music. He's a sculptor.

ANNABELLE: Why did they say all that stuff about your dad for?

TOM: I don't know.

ANNABELLE: They were really, really rude.

TOM: Well, what they said about him is not entirely true.

ANNABELLE: Okay.

TOM: My dad's sculptures are in galleries in Sydney and Melbourne.

ANNABELLE: Wow… that's so great.
TOM: Yeah.
ANNABELLE: You want to go for a walk with me?
TOM: Yeah.
ANNABELLE: Let's go.
They wander off. The music and lights fade.

SCENE THREE

MRS MAC *is in her rocking chair.*

MRS MAC: The girls would swim in a different part of the lake to the boys and we would be all covered up in full piece bathing suits with little skirts around them and caps. [*She laughs.*] Silly caps on our heads to protect our hair… God knows what from!

But it was all still the same, I suppose… still the same then as it is now. When you are young you are young. I remember. I remember it all.

He was a young, tall, strong boy with jet black hair and big shining brown eyes; and he'd swing on the rope from the tree and summersault into the water and every time he did, he'd look across to me; and I knew it was me, and so did everyone else. Some of the girls were scared of him. I never was. He'd swing and smile, and look across to me. You don't forget those things. He didn't seem to care that he was different, that the others would exclude him. He was the tallest and strongest and had the biggest smile without a doubt.

Lights slowly fade on MRS MAC *and come up on* DAD *serving dinner at the table.* TOM *enters and sits down.* DAD *sits and they begin eating in silence.*

DAD: Tom.
TOM: What?
DAD: Why are you smoking pot?
   Silence.
   Tom… why?
TOM: Don't start!
DAD: Why?

TOM: I'm not... okay!
DAD: I found this in your room.

He shows him a bottle bong.

TOM: Well, keep out of my bloody room.
DAD: Well, if you put your washing out once in awhile for me to do... I wouldn't have to go in your bloody room. You used to say that you hated drugs. You said—that—
TOM: Just shut up!
DAD: Don't tell me to shut up, Tom.
TOM: Well, leave me alone then.
DAD: I will not leave you alone. You're not watching your diet at all either. You live on take-away food. This is the first meal you've eaten with me all week. Probably, the first healthy thing that's touched your lips too.
TOM: Yeah... yeah! Would you listen to yourself?
DAD: You know what smoking will do for your chest and breathing, don't you? And your brain; your special, young brain.
TOM: Play a different record will you?
DAD: No... I won't.
TOM: So what else then?
DAD: So! Are you taking your puffer with you?
TOM: Yes!
DAD: You are not! I saw it in your room.
TOM: Keep out my room, please.
DAD: Put your washing out, please.

Silence. They finish eating.

I'm worried about you.
TOM: Don't be.
DAD: You're hurting yourself with the smoking and—how you eat—and—
TOM: No I'm not.

Beat.

DAD: I wish you would talk to me.
TOM: About?
DAD: About everything... about your health.
TOM: Here we go again!

DAD: You don't even go to the doctors anymore to get checked. I made that—appoint—
TOM: Stay out of it… okay!
DAD: Talk to me about why… about anything.
TOM: Anything?
DAD: Yes… anything, at all.
TOM: Blah blah blah… there… anything. Satisfied?
DAD: Don't, Tom.
TOM: Do, Dad.

> *Silence.*

DAD: You keep it all shut up inside; you keep me shut out, and I'm worried.
TOM: I said… don't be… I'm fine.
DAD: You'd tell me if you weren't?
TOM: Yes!

> *Silence.*

DAD: Well, you know that there are counsellors and youth workers in town that you can talk to, don't you?

> *Silence.*

People you can talk to if you don't want to talk to me.

> *Silence.*

Tom… you know that, don't you?
TOM: Yes! Yes I do… alright!
DAD: Good people who are confidential too.

> *Silence.*

They wouldn't say anything to me.

> *Silence.*

It might help if you are worried about something.
TOM: I'm worried about nothing.
DAD: School or friends or smoking dope, whatever is on your mind.

> *They eat.*

I saw you in town walking with a very pretty girl yesterday.
TOM: No, I wasn't.
DAD: Okay… you weren't then… sorry.

They eat in silence.

TOM: Actually... I was.

DAD: Okay... you were.

Silence.

TOM: She's my new friend... Annabelle.

DAD: Is she new in town?

TOM: Yeah... she lives with her mum... and is doing year twelve.

DAD: She might study with you... if you are still finding it difficult.

They eat.

Tom, are you still finding it all too difficult?... Tom?

TOM: I've left.

DAD: What did you say?

TOM: I don't go to school anymore.

DAD: What?

TOM: Don't... okay?

DAD: What do you mean... you've left?

TOM: I hate it.

DAD: But you said—

TOM: Just shut up!

DAD: Don't tell me to shut up!

TOM: And I'm not going back there ever again... and that's just that. I don't want to talk about it anymore.

DAD: Talk to me about it... talk to me about why.

TOM: No!

DAD: Why?

TOM: Just no! Leave me alone.

DAD: You know what we said about year twelve.

TOM: I've left... okay?

DAD: It's just a year of applying yourself, that's all.

TOM: No!

DAD: If you got your year twelve I said I'd give you the money I've been putting away for you... enough for a car.

TOM: No... okay? I'm not doing it... and I'm making my own money.

TOM *leaves the room.*

DAD: Tom!

The lights dim.

Tom, come back here!

Tom! For Christ sake Tom, I feel things too... don't you ever realise... I feel things too.

I feel the pain of watching you hurt yourself. I feel the worry buried deep inside my gut. I feel the guilt at who I am and how I could've been better as a dad, much bloody better. I feel the narrow-mindedness of this town sometimes and the judgments that people made on me because I was just me, that's all, just me; not doing a thing wrong. I'm sorry, Tom; but you need to know I really do feel things too... I do.

The lights go down.

SCENE FOUR

TOM *and* ANNABELLE *are laughing and playing a game. They become arm in arm.*

TOM: My dad went totally off his face.
ANNABELLE: My mum did too.
TOM: What about?
ANNABELLE: About me staying out with you last night... and she said I smelt like pot. I know she smokes pot sometimes herself.
TOM: My dad too, well he used to; they are such hypocrites sometimes.
ANNABELLE: I know.
TOM: You're amazing... you know that.
ANNABELLE: You are too.

They hug and kiss. The lights dim a little on them and come up on MRS MAC, *leaning on her stick.*

MRS MAC: Sometimes when I see the young ones arm in arm I remember that boy from the river, with the big brown eyes and teeth as white as the cotton wool clouds. I remember his smile and the way he snuck around to where I was swimming and dived in. I saw him like a sleek animal slide into the water and then pop his head up next to me. I made out he gave me a terrible fright, but he didn't; my heart jumped for another reason; because he was the most beautiful boy I'd ever seen. I didn't understand the way he made me feel; the nights I would lay in bed thinking of him; him, my boy from the lake. My beautiful boy from the lake.

The lights dim on MRS MAC *and the lights go up on* TOM *and* ANNABELLE.

TOM: You're beautiful.

ANNABELLE: You are too.

They kiss.

I wish we had some where we could go just together… don't you? There are too many other kids around here.

TOM: Well… I kind of have.

ANNABELLE: Where?

TOM: I never took anyone there before.

ANNABELLE: Where is it?

TOM: I've never even told anyone about it before either.

ANNABELLE: What Tom?

TOM: You'll think I'm stupid.

ANNABELLE: No I won't.

TOM: It's really just an old shed near a church.

ANNABELLE: [*laughing*] Take me there… please!

TOM: It's kind of been my special, private place since I was a little kid. I fixed the holes in the roof and put some stuff in there.

ANNABELLE: Please take me there.

TOM: Okay. Come on then.

They wander off, arm in arm, talking and laughing. The lights come up on the shed, where ANNABELLE *and* TOM *are kissing.*

TOM: I call it the Yum Yum Room.

ANNABELLE: The Yum Yum Room?

TOM: Yep… that's what I call it.

ANNABELLE: The Yum Yum Room! That's really cute, Tom. Why do you call it that?

TOM: Actually… because I use to always eat tons of lollies and chocolates in here. Then I smoked cigarettes in here for awhile… that's all; and my dad wouldn't let me eat lollies too much, and would go absolutely mental if he knew I smoked.

ANNABELLE: I hate cigarettes! They stink and are disgusting and give you lung cancer.

TOM: I know! And now, I just come here just 'cos I want to hang out here by myself and enjoy myself… like lollies… like a bong… like Yum bloody yum!
ANNABELLE: Tommy Yum Yum. Tommy bloody Yum Yum. That's what I'll call you.

They laugh and kiss.

TOM: No! The Yum Yum Room. Not me. It's called… this place is called the Yum Yum Room.

They kiss.

SCENE FIVE

DAD *is putting food out on the table.* ANNABELLE *and* TOM *come in, sit at the table and start eating.*

ANNABELLE: Tom showed me one of your sculptures in your studio. I love it. I love it so much.
DAD: Thanks Annabelle. What time are you two going out?
TOM: When we've finished this.
DAD: If you take the car… you must not have one drink, Tom… not one. You know with P-plates that you can't.
TOM: I know!
ANNABELLE: I'll make sure he won't… Tom doesn't really ever drink anyway.
DAD: Do you Annabelle?
ANNABELLE: Sometimes; but not really that much.
DAD: Do you smoke pot like he does?
ANNABELLE: No.
DAD: You should take some notice of Annabelle, Tom.
ANNABELLE: I can't really study if I do.
DAD: Have you talked to him about going back to school?
ANNABELLE: He won't.
TOM: Nup… I won't. And Dad smokes pot too.
DAD: Did!
TOM: And he goes on and on at me… which I don't think is that fair actually.
DAD: I've stopped now. And I've told you how years of doing that leaves you with a nasty long-term habit, bad lungs and brain

damage; like me probably… I don't want that for you, Tom. I want better; I think I'm off it for good; don't let anyone tell you that the pot is not addictive. It's bloody bad for you, that stuff. I want the best for you, mate; better than what's been for me… much better.

TOM: I reckon parents are so bloody hypocritical sometimes.

DAD: Stop saying bloody all the time.

TOM: No.

DAD: I do too… hypocritical I mean; I can hear myself sometimes, and I know it's bloody ridiculous, but I mean it; I don't just say it for fun.

ANNABELLE: My mum is too. She goes out drinking and partying all night… and when I do… it's another story… always.

DAD: She probably just cares about you very much.

ANNABELLE: I know.

DAD: Wants better for you too! None of us are perfect.

ANNABELLE: I know.

TOM: I'm going to have a really quick shower before we go.

ANNABELLE: Okay.

He exits.

DAD: Here's the photo you wanted to see.

ANNABELLE: He's so cute. How old is he there?

DAD: Four.

ANNABELLE: You and Tom seem to get on really well.

DAD: You think that?

ANNABELLE: Yeah.

DAD: All we ever seem to do is argue now days.

ANNABELLE: He thinks a lot of you.

DAD: I wonder sometimes.

ANNABELLE: He always talks about you and your sculptures.

DAD: Really?

ANNABELLE: Yes.

DAD: I haven't always been the best dad.

ANNABELLE: I think you probably have been.

DAD: Thanks Annabelle… but no, no I haven't.

ANNABELLE: I know that some of the kids have given him crap about you… said all these really cruel things, about you.

DAD: I know that. They made it very hard for him at one stage.
ANNABELLE: I know it's probably all bullshit though, what they say.
DAD: Maybe or may not be. You can ask me.

Silence.

You can.
ANNABELLE: Are you gay?
DAD: I really am the ideal dad, aren't I?
ANNABELLE: Probably you are. You don't have to answer me. It's rude of me to say that actually.

Silence.

Are you?
DAD: Well, I had a relationship for a year with a very special guy from Perth who was teaching here… about five years ago, and we kept it quiet, but it got out and… well, you know this town. Well, you probably don't yet.
ANNABELLE: No… I do.
DAD: All the fuss about him and me died down after awhile though. But he left… my friend. The school made it difficult for him. The parents; the other teachers. But poor old Tom was only about eleven or twelve and all the kids gave him so much crap. Still do I think! People can be very hostile when they don't understand, when they discriminate because of fear or whatever.
TOM: [*entering*] What's he raving on about?
ANNABELLE: He's not raving on.
TOM: Come on… let's go. See you, Dad.
DAD: See you, mate.
ANNABELLE: See you, Dad… Tom's dad!
DAD: See you, Annabelle… Tom's Annabelle.

They exit, but ANNABELLE *comes back in.*

ANNABELLE: And I do think you are a good dad. [*She kisses him on the cheek.*] And there's nothing wrong with being gay, if that's how you are.

She exits.

DAD: Thanks Annabelle.

SCENE SIX

MRS MAC sits in her rocking chair.

MRS MAC: I knew it would never be possible with my beautiful boy, back there, back then; of course not; even though I loved him and he loved me, back then it was different. Although I don't know; people are still a bit funny about things they fear, things they don't understand or agree with. We would meet, my boy and me, at a special place at the lake and it was like we were in heaven when we were together. We would swim and laugh and joke and make up stories about how we would wander the countryside together forever and ever and never worry about anything or anyone else. And we would kiss in a special place I had just for me… we would kiss and hold each other as the sun went down. But someone told my parents about seeing me with him and after that, after something my dad and the priest and the school and the police said to him he went away. Just like that… he went away. They sent him away, and I didn't even know where he went. I cried for months. His name was Tom too. But my Tom was an aboriginal boy with his big brown eyes and fine white teeth, and I was a white girl, and that was back in the nineteen fifties and well that was that then… back then. But we loved each other; we really, really loved each other; my brown-eyed Tom and me. And they should've never sent him away… never ever.

TOM is talking on his mobile phone in the shed.

TOM: Well, where are you then?… You said that tonight it definitely wouldn't be a problem going out… I know that, but that's what you said to me… Well, you lied to me then!

MRS MAC: He's been going into his Yum Yum Room with Annabelle the last few weeks.

TOM: I have been here fucking waiting for you, Annabelle… You said!

MRS MAC: But not today… or yesterday… or the day before either.

TOM: Why?

MRS MAC: The pretty, pretty girl called Annabelle whose mother works in the clinic in town.

TOM: But you said that yesterday too.

MRS MAC: I think he is probably in love with her… Annabelle. A special, young love.

THE YUM YUM ROOM

TOM: Well, I didn't see you yesterday or the day before.
MRS MAC: But I'm just not too sure if she is love with him.
TOM: But why?
MRS MAC: An old woman knows these things.
TOM: Why, Annabelle?
MRS MAC: And sees things too.
TOM: I thought we were going to borrow Dad's car and drive to Millicent on the week end.
MRS MAC: Maybe I should say to him… Tom, Tommy boy, I don't want to see you hurt.
TOM: I have been sitting here bloody waiting… well, you said!

>TOM *puts down the phone, and holds his head in his hands.*

MRS MAC: I've watched you, Tom… for many years; and we've had a cup of tea together here and there, spoken and laughed. But I saw Annabelle, the pretty thing she is. I saw her bring a boy… another boy… she bought another boy into the Yum Yum Room… your Yum Yum Room, Tom, late the other night… without you.
TOM: [*screaming*] No!
MRS MAC: And I wanted to go in there and say, what do you think you are doing bringing someone in to the Yum Yum Room? He trusted you.
TOM: I trusted you!
MRS MAC: He shared his place with you.
TOM: I shared my place with you… I shared everything with you, Annabelle.
MRS MAC: She was kissing the same other boy last Wednesday in the car park of Lake Village too.
TOM: No!
MRS MAC: I saw her. Maybe Tom… it is not for her like it is for you, not like it seems.

>TOM *screams and throws something in the shed.*

But what can an old woman say?

>*Blackout. Lights go up on* TOM *with his mobile.*

TOM: [*angrily*] And you didn't even tell me. That other kid had to. That other kid who is probably your boyfriend now. [*Screaming*] Why?

>TOM *wanders back to the shed. He picks up a bong and a can of beer.*

[*Screaming*] Why?

MRS MAC: He knows now. I can hear him in there, but I stay away... I don't want to stay away, but I do.

> *Lights dim on* MRS MAC *and come up on* DAD *in the kitchen.* TOM *stands in the Yum Yum Room, holding a bong and a beer.*

DAD: He is in a world I am not allowed to enter.

TOM: How could you do that to me, Annabelle?

DAD: Tom.

TOM: I loved you!

DAD: The poor, poor kid.

> DAD *and* TOM *face each other.*

TOM: It's got nothing to do with you.

DAD: It's Annabelle, isn't it?

TOM: No... okay... no! It's probably your fault anyway.

DAD: Is it my fault... is it? Tom, why are you saying that to me?

TOM: You; how you are.

DAD: I'm sorry.

TOM: Just forget it... just leave me alone, will you?

> *They turn away from each other.*

DAD: I am on the fringe of everything that means anything to me and I am shut out.

TOM: Bloody leave me alone.

DAD: I bloody care.

TOM: Everyone bloody leave me alone forever.

DAD: I am awake when he is not here... waiting... worried and shaken by how much I care about what my Tom is feeling.

TOM: It's not really your fault. She's just a fucking bitch... that's all. I hate her so, so much.

DAD: You're drunk mate.

TOM: I am not bloody drunk!

DAD: You're drunk and stoned.

TOM: Big deal... okay!

DAD: It's not going to help anything.

TOM: You're a fine one to talk anyway.

DAD: I know that.

TOM: It's got nothing to do with you.

DAD: Sometimes you just have to try to…
TOM: What the hell would you know, anyway?
DAD: I do know, Tom.
TOM: You don't know anything.
> *Silence.*
> Just shut up.
> *Silence.*
> You're bloody gay anyway.

DAD: Well yes… yes I am, Tom. But there are some things that I do know.
> *Silence.*
> I know hurt too; I understand.
> *Silence.*

TOM: Leave me alone.
DAD: I know what it's like to be left by someone I loved… even though others may not understand. I know what it's like to worry all day and night about someone whose life means more to me than my own. Don't do anything silly, Tom.
TOM: I might.
DAD: Tom.
TOM: I bloody won't.
> MRS MAC *leans on her stick.*

MRS MAC: I would like to tell him that I am here.
> TOM *stands still in the shed.*
> Tom.
> *They face each other.*

TOM: Yes.
MRS MAC: Would you like to come in and have a cup of tea with me?
TOM: [*walking to* MRS MAC] No thanks… I'm going down the street. It's Thursday night.
MRS MAC: Okay… that's okay then. You go off and enjoy yourself.
TOM: Mrs Mac?
MRS MAC: Yes, my boy?
TOM: I can't enjoy myself… anymore… ever again.
MRS MAC: Why?

TOM: Because I just can't… that's why. Because I trusted someone who ran off and left me. And I know that shit. I really know that shit. Is that what everyone does… to me? Is that what women do? Is that how it is in this life?
MRS MAC: Not always, Tom.
TOM: A big hole in my life.
MRS MAC: It won't always be like that.
TOM: A big hole in heart. It's probably that. [*He wheezes a little and uses his puffer.*] Or my stupid asthma. Or my stupid mother who ran away from me too.
MRS MAC: I don't think so, but if it was, well we wouldn't worry about someone like Annabelle then, would we?
TOM: I don't know. Probably because my stupid dad is gay.
MRS MAC: I don't think so, about that either. He's okay… your dad.
TOM: I know he is.
MRS MAC: It will not always seem so bad.
TOM: For me it will.
MRS MAC: It may seem like that now, but really it won't.
TOM: Everyone thinks they know everything.
MRS MAC: I was in love once when I was young… and he left.
TOM: Really?
MRS MAC: Yes. It wasn't his fault. It was a stupid narrow view of the world of other people, of discrimination and narrow-mindedness… that sent him away… away from me.
TOM: That's shit Mrs Mac. It really is.
MRS MAC: I got over it eventually.
TOM: How?
MRS MAC: Looked for all the other things in my life that were special; that meant something; and talked about it too… I had a special friend and when I needed to not feel so alone… I talked about it to her.
TOM: I don't want to ever talk to anyone about it, ever!
MRS MAC: Well you just talked to me.

    Silence.

TOM: Yeah… I did.
MRS MAC: Don't keep it all bottled up, Tom… to yourself.

TOM: Thank you, Mrs Mac.
MRS MAC: You come in here anytime you want.
TOM: Okay.
MRS MAC: And you have got your dad. And whatever, he is your dad and he cares very much about you.
TOM: I know.

    TOM *moves away.*

My dad and me went out for dinner at the pub the other night. We don't usually do that; but he asked me to and I thought, yeah… why not? I'm not really that ashamed of Dad. I used to think I was, but it doesn't seem as big as it once was. Lots of people in town actually like my dad, and lots of people at the pub talked with him and said hello.

DAD: I said… please, my mate; let's have dinner together. I won't go on and on at you, like I do.
TOM: Don't okay! I don't want to talk about it!
DAD: [*moving to* TOM] No… we'll just have dinner and talk about… about…
TOM: That kid I know who is in trouble with the cops.
DAD: Your hip-hop music… and how you still want to be a DJ.
TOM: I'm pleased you got a nomination for an art prize.
DAD: Yeah?
TOM: Yeah. Of course I am.

    They drift away from each other.

And he didn't go on and on at me to talk to him about Annabelle.
DAD: I bit my tongue and tried to just enjoy the time together.
TOM: And I did tell him in my time.

    They move together again.

Annabelle left me for some other stupid guy and that's that and I don't want to go on and on about it.
DAD: Okay mate… okay.

    They move away from each other.

And we talked more about his hip-hop music and the job at McDonald's.
TOM: And he just said that if I needed him for anything…
DAD: Anything at all, mate… I am always here.

TOM: And I know he is. But sometimes you got to find the right people to talk to about the right things. It's not all as simple as... just talking to someone. It was kind of easier to talk to Mrs Mac about that than it was Dad. I don't know why... but it just was.

The other afternoon I was alone and I hated myself and my life so much. I feel like such a bloody fool. I feel so cheated and like I am the most stupid guy on earth, and how Annabelle is probably laughing at me with her new guy right now; and the kids they hang around with would be too; and this stupid life where I've been left by my mum and the first girl I ever loved; left with a big gaping hole in my life... again, like the big gaping hole in my heart.

She was so special to me.

I didn't want to go back to the Yum Yum Room... ever. She even changed the way I felt about there. So I go to work instead, at McDonald's... I go to work for my DJ stuff. I will be a bloody DJ. Nothing will stop me doing that! I was walking around the other day, and I started to feel like total crap again. Not just Annabelle, but Mum too and knowing that the dope makes me feel worse not better, but not giving it up because I'm so bloody pissed off with everything; and then I saw this youth worker dude, who I know from when I went to The Loft one night with some other kids, and he asked me how I was; and I talked to him for awhile about all that crap going on in my mind; Annabelle, Dad being gay, the dope and my stupid mum who I really, really do remember well, but make out to myself that I don't. He was pretty cool, this youth worker dude; and sitting down talking to him I did feel better; like I do when I talk to Mrs Mac or even my crazy old dad. But with him... well, he didn't know me much and it was kind of easier. I think I'm going to stay off the dope for now; I'll see how I go anyway. Dad gave it away; I bet I can too. And I don't feel so bloody confused as when I'm smoking it. I suppose I'm kind of lucky really. There are a few people I can talk to; but not Annabelle. I won't talk to Annabelle ever again!

ANNABELLE *is in the background.*

ANNABELLE: I'm so sorry, Tom... really I am.

TOM: [*to the audience*] Not ever! And that's my decision. She really hurt me. But today I'm feeling even better than yesterday... and today... I might even go back to the Yum Yum Room.

MRS MAC: [*from her chair*] That's the way, Tommy boy.
TOM: Yep… the bloody Yum Yum Room.
DAD: Your Yum Yum Room. It will always be your Yum Yum Room. I love you Tom.
TOM: I know you do Dad. I always know you do. [*Quietly*] Me too.
MRS MAC: [*laughing*] The Yum Yum Room.

THE END

Crowded House
John Romeril

Photograph: Kanamori Mayu

JOHN ROMERIL began his playwriting career while a Monash University undergraduate with *I Don't Know Who to Feel Sorry For* (1969) and *Chicago, Chicago* (1969–70). Romeril helped found the APG in 1970 and many of his plays of the period, including *Mrs Thally F*, *Bastardy*, *The Floating World* and *Carboni* premiered there. His other plays include (from the 1980s) *Samizdat*, *Jonah*, *Legends*, *Lost Weekend*, *Top End* and *Koori Radio*. The 1990s saw his continued success with *Black Cargo*, *Crowded House*, *Reading Boy*, *Doing the Block*, *Expo: The Human Factor*, *Acronetic*, *Kate 'n' Shiner*, *Love Suicides* and *Hanoi-Melbourne*. *Miss Tanaka* premiered at Playbox in 2001 and his stage adaptation of *One Night the Moon* at Malthouse in 2009.

His screen credits include *The Great McCarthy*, *Six of the Best* (a 12-part series for ABC) and, with Rachel Perkins, *One Night the Moon* (2000).

He has been Playwright-in-Residence with a number of theatre companies and tertiary institutions. Prizes include the Canada-Australia Literary Award (1976), and the Patrick White Award (2008).

The cast of the 1992 Arena production. (Photograph: The Arts Centre, Performing Arts Collection, Melbourne, Trina Parker Collection.)

Crowded House was first produced as *Bring Down The House* by Arena for the Next Wave Festival. It first toured in May 1992 before being produced at Malthouse Theatre, Playbox, Melbourne, on 20 May 1992 with the following cast:

WILL	David Adamson
FRIEDA	Phillipa Adgemis
RITA	Kim Trengove
MORG	Richard Davies

Director, Barbara Ciszewska
Designer, Trina Parker
Lighting Designer, Liz Pain
Musical Direction, Irene Vela

CHARACTERS
FRIEDA
WILL
MORG
RITA

GIRL
SOCIAL WORKER
DARYL
EUNICE
PAUL
DELPHIE
JOHN
ALDISS
TESS
ROSE

The play is written for four actors, two male, two female.

SETTING and MUSIC

Apart from a riot at the start, and escape bid at the end, the action of *Crowded House* occurs inside a house. Trina Parker built an inner city Victorian era terrace house circa 1890s Melbourne—but to a doll's house scale. She set that model on stage, adding a rigid steel joist, something you might see in the debris of a demolition site. It was load-bearing, and though made of wood, gave actors an elevated position to perform from at times. Two or three bound bundles of newspapers were provided, also for performers to stand or sit on. Arena had touring to schools in mind. Scenic items had to fit in a van, be swiftly erected and taken down.

Music was a mix of found sound, popular songs that gave chapters of the show an era feel, eg. 1930s dance hall tunes, 1960s rock'n'roll. For the riot actors worked 'live' to pre-recorded crowd sound effects. For the *Crowded House* lyrics, musical director Irine Vela drilled the performers to deliver it in hip-hop a capella fashion.

SCENE ONE

A heavy urgent sound track begins: the underscore for a riot some time in the near future. Chants like 'Eat the rich!', 'Hold the line!' and 'The whole world's watching' are mixed in. Searchlights and flares come up to reveal a smoke-wreathed stage. Mayhem and confusion reign. Two women enter slowly and separately. FRIEDA *is moving through a press of bodies.* RITA *is hunching against a wall, wearing a rucksack. Just as slowly,* WILL *and* MORG *are entering. They're together.*

FRIEDA: There's smoke. Screams. Fear and confusion. A crowd pressing in. Bodies crushing up against you. People galore. But not one of 'em knows what to do.

   Focus shifts to WILL *and* MORG.

WILL: We have rights. The inalienable rights all humans have.

MORG: Get this through your head: there are no rights. They've turned off the rights.

   Focus shifts to RITA.

RITA: I get through it saying: this is a music-pub. This is a crowded hall. I tell myself people are dancing, not being gassed; the ones falling down have drunk too much.

   Focus shifts back to WILL *and* MORG.

WILL: People think I'm mad.

MORG: You are mad.

WILL: What's my madness compared to the madness of all this?

MORG: Duck!

   They shield themselves.

FRIEDA: The sweepers are coming through, firing cannisters. The god squad with their riot shields and stun guns won't be far behind. Could even be waiting for us up ahead. We're like rats herded through a maze, being driven deeper into the old part of the city.

WILL: This slaughter of the innocents must cease!

FRIEDA: The police dogs get fed—the people don't. Strange the things you think.

RITA: You see a face in the crowd—you'd like to trust that person but who can you trust? You'd like a friend, somebody to care if you live or die.
FRIEDA: Hey you!
RITA: She grabs me.
FRIEDA: I know a way out of here.
RITA: I pretend it's a dance.
FRIEDA: I know this part of town.
RITA: Somebody's asked me to dance.

> RITA *and* FRIEDA *join up.* WILL *pushes forward.*

WILL: I will speak to my enemies. I am Usoffa leading you from this wilderness. They will see reason.
MORG: Will!
WILL: I will give them the chance to negotiate a solution.
MORG: Will!
WILL: I will give them a window of opportunity.
MORG: A lobotomy's what you'll get. A slug to the frontal lobes. Not that way.

> WILL *has been hit. His leg buckles.* MORG *goes to aid him. A crowd forms.*

WILL: Argh!
MORG: See what I mean!
WILL: What happened to my leg?
MORG: Stun gun.
WILL: Stun gun?
MORG: [*yelling*] Hot wire!
RITA: I pretend I'm at a gig, in a video-clip. I pretend I'm listening to a band—that all this is coming out of a karaoke machine!
SONG: When there's trouble in the street it's calling your name.
You think you'll cop a bullet and you can't cope.
You're sick of copping the blame.
When trouble—like a rope—tightens around you.
It's not a slip knot it's a noose.
Someone you dunno who wants to cook your goose.
What's the point you're thinking.
What's the point you're thinking.

What's the point/What's the point?
What's the use?

    RITA *and* FRIEDA *take focus.*

RITA: Why's this happening?

FRIEDA: What have you heard?

RITA: That young people are surplus to requirements. That it's the final solution.

FRIEDA: That's what I've heard.

RITA: How can that make sense?

FRIEDA: Who knows? But it's happening.

    The song continues.

SONG: Behind you the bridge is burning.
    No way back across the river.
    To the left and right the roads are blocked.
    No way through to the port.
    Overhead you can hear planes still leaving the airfield.
    But no vacant seats—every ticket's been bought.
    No way to vamoose.
    What's the point you're thinking.
    What's the point you're thinking.
    What's the point/What's the point?
    What's the use?

    The flares and searchlights reach a climax and quiet begins to return.

SCENE TWO

The front window of an abandoned house are boarded up with sheet iron and timbers. RITA *and* FRIEDA *enter.*

FRIEDA: Is it your eyes?

RITA: My lips and cheeks.

FRIEDA: Blisters?

RITA: They sting.

FRIEDA: Don't use water. Spreads it worse. The sting goes. They're using a new sort of gas. Leaves pock marks, see, like these.

    FRIEDA *shows* RITA *her scars.*

RITA: Yuck.
FRIEDA: Worried you won't look beautiful?
RITA: How do I look?
FRIEDA: The way I feel.
RITA: Awful.
FRIEDA: Scared. Here.

>FRIEDA *tosses* RITA *a tube.*

Salve. Kind of ointment. Might save your skin a bit.
RITA: Why are you giving it to me?
FRIEDA: I like you.
RITA: You hardly know me.
FRIEDA: Okay, you dragged me into a doorway when the sweepers went through.
RITA: You did that for me.
FRIEDA: So I got a bad memory and think I owe you one. Maybe I can't stand seeing people in pain.
RITA: Thanks.
FRIEDA: That's a word you don't hear too often. You for staying out here or finding somewhere safer?
RITA: Where's safe these days?

>FRIEDA *indicates the house behind her.*

You think the people living here boarded the window up and left?
FRIEDA: Dunno.
RITA: You think the people living here boarded it up cos they were jack of having the joint broken into?
FRIEDA: Dunno.
RITA: They wouldn't still be living here, would they?
FRIEDA: Only one way to find out, eh?

>FRIEDA *uses a jemmy to bash the iron. The following sequence develops as a song.*

FRIEDA: When you break into a house—
RITA: When you're on the run—
FRIEDA: When you need a place for the night—
RITA: Cos you're on the run—
FRIEDA: When you're thinking this'll do—
RITA: It will—have to—You—
FRIEDA: Look back—

RITA: The way you've come.
FRIEDA: Anyone watching you?
RITA: Anyone clocking you?
FRIEDA: Anyone on your tail?

> *The lowered sheet iron forms a slide. They climb down it into the room.*

RITA: Empty houses scare me.
FRIEDA: It's when they're not empty they worry me.
RITA: What now?
FRIEDA: We put the pieces back and hope nobody notices the difference. Too late.
RITA: What?
FRIEDA: Voices.

> *They melt into the shadows.*

FRIEDA: When you break into a house —
RITA: When you're on the run—
FRIEDA: You're in through the window—
RITA: Melting like a shadow—
FRIEDA: Sinking like a setting sun—
RITA: Freeze.
FRIEDA: A picture.
RITA: Freeze.
FRIEDA: A statue.
RITA: To one side.
FRIEDA: Some are born to live but some—
RITA: To live must hide.

> RITA *and* FRIEDA *freeze.* WILL *and* MORG *appear.*

MORG: Not that way. Wake up to yourself.
WILL: I am permanently awake.
MORG: Go that way you'll be permanently asleep.
WILL: Cryogenics. The science of freezing the dead in order to restore life at a later stage.
MORG: What I like about you, your light breezy conversational touch. Get in.
WILL: What's the point the sweepers have got infra-red sensors? They'll flush us out.
MORG: They mightn't come this way. I said: get in.

> MORG *lifts/pushes* WILL *down the slide.*

When you break into a house,
WILL: When you need a place for the night,
MORG: When you're thinking this'll do,
WILL: It will—have to—You,
MORG: Look back,
WILL: The way you've come.
MORG: Anyone watching you?
WILL: Anyone clocking you?
MORG: Anyone on your tail?

> MORG *is in the house now.*

I had a brother like you.
WILL: What happened to him?
MORG: He died.
WILL: You killed him.
MORG: They took him away.
WILL: Put him in a mental institution?
MORG: It was the best thing for everyone.

> *Women add 'ghost' harmonies, echoes to the song.*

When you break into a house,
WILL: When you're on the run,
MORG: You're in through the window,
WILL: Melting like a shadow,
MORG: Sinking like a setting sun.
WILL: Freeze you're,
MORG: A picture.
WILL: Freeze you're,
MORG: A statue.
WILL: Off to one side.
MORG: Some are born to live but some,
WILL: To live must hide.

> *They look around the place.*

I don't like it here.
MORG: You got a better idea, Brains Trust?

> FRIEDA *steps out of hiding.*

FRIEDA: Try down the road.
MORG: Company.
WILL: There could be dancing.
MORG: Two against one.
WILL: Hip. Hop.
RITA: You can go back the way you came.
MORG: Two against two.
WILL: Looks like there will be dancing. Hop hip.

    FRIEDA *looks menacing with her jemmy.*

RITA: Are you two on the run?
WILL: Are we on the run?
FRIEDA: Tell 'em nothing.
RITA: We are.
FRIEDA: State your business.
MORG: Any port in a storm.
FRIEDA: This port's ours.
MORG: We've sailed through the heads. Any chance bed and breakfast?
FRIEDA: None whatever.
WILL: Quiet!

    WILL, *dervish-like, spins out, then pauses.*

MORG: He's listening.
RITA: To what?
WILL: The house.
MORG: Walls buildings staircases—they talk to him.
WILL: I hear my voice.
FRIEDA: That's cos you're talking.
WILL: I've been here before.
FRIEDA: What's he on?
MORG: What he's not on is the problem. Haven't had a green? Have a green. Have a red. Have two reds. Have the whole medicine chest amigo.

    MORG *offers a satchel to* WILL, *who ignores the offer.*

Don't want your medicine? Fine. I'll sell it to someone who does. I am not my brother's keeper.
WILL: The walls. They're talking to me, same as they did when I was here last time.

MORG: When you—were here last time?
WILL: I used to live here.
MORG: Give me a break you schitzed out piece of street trash.
WILL: I do. Did. I was a kid, twelve. I got placed here. A danger to myself, they said. It was a welfare house, they said, a halfway house.
MORG: A refuge? It still is. A refuge—for us.
WILL: This place used to be okay.
FRIEDA: So was Australia.
WILL: In 1992 I was here.
RITA: Was he?
MORG: Could be. I've no way of knowing.
WILL: It was a crowded house, a very crowded house.

Transformation to 1992 begins.

There was a girl there. In the corner.

FRIEDA *to one side plays the girl.*

Always watching television. Dawn to dawn. Catatonic. She never spoke.
GIRL: Or did you never listen?
WILL: She had a strange aura but I trusted her. And one of the social workers we had, I trusted him.

MORG *plays the social worker.*

WORKER: You need a lot of help, you realise.
WILL: That's why I'm here. I need help. They had welfare then.
WORKER: You've been robbed of a lot of basic functions, haven't you.
WILL: And I know why. The planet is run by the Third Reich.
WORKER: You need to re-learn a great number of things.
WILL: I need lessons in humanity.
WORKER: Do you know how to shower?
WILL: No.
WORKER: How to blow your nose?
WILL: No.
WORKER: We'll teach you all sorts of things, how to cook for yourself, how to budget for rent, electricity, food—so you'll be able to take your place in society.
WILL: I was happy here except—
WORKER: The government's backed down.

WILL: Government had been going to finance the house.
WORKER: Local council's also got cold feet.
WILL: Council had been going to help.
WORKER: The welfare state's being wound down.
WILL: The social worker fired us up. We held meetings. Wrote letters. We'll fight it.
WORKER: If you're gonna do that you better start by gathering petitions.
WILL: That's when I met the neighbours.
RITA: Met who? Who'd he meet?
WILL: The neighbours.

    RITA *plays a neighbour.*

NEIGHBOUR: I'm not signing that.
WILL: The neighbours didn't like us.
NEIGHBOUR: We want their kind out of there.
WILL: Didn't want us in institutions, didn't want us in houses either.
NEIGHBOUR: They're driving property values down.
WILL: Crowded house.
RITA: He's off again.
WILL: Crowded house.
MORG: He'll come back to us.
WILL: Sooner or later. Generation after generation. Everyone living in this house gets it in the neck. Even the girl who never spoke, spoke.
GIRL: Blast some sense into 'em I say!
NEIGHBOUR: And they play loud music!

    Sound level of crowded house ascends.

WILL: When we saw the way things were, the forces against us—
WORKER: They've stopped paying my wage.
WILL: We played music non-stop, the same tune, for thirty-eight days till the lease ran out!

    'Crowded House' lyric starts.

SONG: Hanging by a thread swinging on a strand,
    No supply despite demand,
    No supply and nothing planned,
    What used to be a city's now a village of the dammed,
    We feed on rumour fuelled by hate,
    What's not in hock is on the slate,

Here for the party and we can't wait,
Whatcha mean its over and we're too late,
Nothing shouted nothing said,
But a whisper in your head,
It's a crowded house,
A crowded house,
A crowded house.

Characters develop a hip-hop routine.

One day in Pompeii should have been a clue,
Or you're in Tokyo an earthquake's overdue,
Cairo's a jungle, LA a zoo,
San Francisco's on a faultline poor little you,
Everywhere's a rat's nest,
Everywhere's a rat's nest,
A python's coming through,
It's a crowded house,
A crowded house,
A crowded house,
Homeland fatherland motherland hearth,
It's a crowded house,
A crowded house,
A crowded house.

WILL *keeps dancing and music continues, but the reality of 1992 fades for the others.*

FRIEDA: That what you get out of this? The laughs?
MORG: The laughs are few and far between.
FRIEDA: Your own dancing monkey.
MORG: I'll pretend I didn't hear that.
WILL: We should have fought harder, we could have fought harder.
FRIEDA: Or is it a sexual thing?
MORG: What?
FRIEDA: What's he like in the shower?
MORG: What's your scene?
FRIEDA: Just wondering why you look after him.
MORG: He's not much chop at looking after himself.
FRIEDA: You don't have to do it.

MORG: Someone does. Are you volunteering?
FRIEDA: What's in it for you?

> WILL *sings.*

WILL: In 1992.
In 1992.
They'll still be watering down the milk.
In 1992.

> *The music continues.*

MORG: Whatcha hearing?
WILL: Sheet music. It's a song.
MORG: From 1992?
WILL: From 1932. A family gathered round a piano in this room and sang that song. The piano was over there. And every Friday night father would come home with the latest tune—him, his wife, the two kids, a happy family would sing, altogether now. The walls. They're telling me what their favourite novelty song was.
FRIEDA: Is he for real?
WILL: A bit later, only the kids. The place she's standing, a woman, young woman, the daughter, keeled over.
RITA: Sure.
WILL: 1932. Height of the Great Depression. She hit the deck. Malnutrition. She hadn't eaten for days. I haven't either.

> RITA *sinks to the floor.*

SCENE THREE

RITA *becomes* EUNICE *and* MORG *becomes her brother* DARYL. WILL *and* FRIEDA *freeze by the window. They will enter the action as* PAUL *and* DELPHIE. *A foxtrot tune will run through the scene.*

DARYL: Eunice!
EUNICE: I'm alright. I just haven't eaten for days.
DARYL: Oh where is father?
FRIEDA: The father who used to bring sheet music home on Friday nights?
EUNICE: And mother.
WILL: Who cooked such amazing apple pies?

DARYL: Why did they leave?
EUNICE: To help with the fruit harvest on our relatives' farm.
DARYL: But why, why?
EUNICE: They're trying to keep the family together.
DARYL: By leaving us?

> EUNICE *rises, and dances with* DARYL.

EUNICE: Slow slow, quick quick,
Slow slow, quick quick.
DARYL: Yesterday the bailiffs came to repossess the piano. Today, the landlord—look, it's a notice of eviction.

> *He shows her the notice. She rips it up.*

EUNICE: I've had an idea.
DARYL: Slow slow, quick quick.
EUNICE: Slow slow, quick quick. You and I.
DARYL: You're so pale.
EUNICE: You and I will enter tonight's—slow slow, quick quick—competition at Leggets Ballroom.
DARYL: How can you even think of ballroom dancing!

> *He stops dancing. She doesn't.*

EUNICE: Slow slow, quick quick.
DARYL: Slow's right, how time drags when you spend all day chasing work at every menswear store in Chapel Street.
EUNICE: How was Chapel Street?
DARYL: Nothing doing.
EUNICE: It's the Depression. Slow slow, quick quick.
DARYL: Yesterday, the bailiffs. Today the landlord.
EUNICE: But tonight: the competition, don't you see! First prize a Chevrolet car, valued at five hundred and seventy five pounds.
DARYL: Of course! I'm so thick.
EUNICE: That way we'll save our family's bacon!

> WILL *becomes* PAUL, FRIEDA *becomes* DELPHIE.

PAUL: If bacon's the go I'll have some!
DARYL: Paul!
PAUL: Yes. Fresh from traipsing the backblocks of Australia looking for work and guess what: there isn't any.
EUNICE: Paul, our old neighbourhood pal.

DARYL: My boyhood idol!
EUNICE: My childhood sweetheart!
PAUL: My wife.
DELPH: Delphie's the name.
EUNICE: Your wife?
PAUL: Met her in Queensland.
EUNICE: You're married?
PAUL: Hunting a job cutting cane. Do you think I could land one?
DELPH: But he did land me!

    PAUL *gestures in a cane-cutting motion.* EUNICE *falls yet again.*

What's wrong with her? And the house?
DARYL: She hasn't eaten for days.
DELPH: I smell tragedy.
PAUL: The furniture—where's it gone?
DARYL: Repossessed. Plus the landlord's evicting us.
PAUL: Only one answer, eh Delph?
DELPH: We've seen this before.
PAUL: You get together with your neighbours.
DELPH: They barricade their houses and you barricade yours.
PAUL: Together you stage a rent strike.
DARYL: Strike?
PAUL: You all refuse to pay your rent.
DELPH: And if the landlords don't listen to that, you strike—
PAUL: A match.

    They strike matches.

And torch the street a house at a time. The landlords pretty soon get the message.

    EUNICE *gets to her feet.*

EUNICE: We prefer doing it our way.
PAUL: What way's that, princess?
EUNICE: Slow slow—
DARYL: Quick quick.
EUNICE: Slow slow—
DARYL: Quick quick.
EUNICE: And the entry fee won't be a problem, Daryl. Look: our last five shillings.

DARYL: We'll win the competition.
EUNICE: We'll drive away in the Chevrolet.

> *Lights fade on* EUNICE *and* DARYL *dancing as the song 'Over the Hill' is sung as they return to the present.*

SONG: On the other side of the hill,
  The sun is always shining,
  On the other side of the hill,
  There'll be an end to pining,
  When we stand on the top of the hill,
  If we've been givers not takers,
  We'll see the golden acres,
  On the other side of the hill.
FRIEDA: And did they win?
WILL: Course not. For someone to get something for next to nothing a lot of people have to get nothing for something. Tragedy. This house has known nothing but. Depression. Recession. Idiocy. And that will be our lot too. Winners and losers. A site for tragedy and a tragic sight. That's what this house has always been.

SCENE FOUR

WILL—*shades again of a dervish—writhes and twists, muttering and groaning as though possessed.*

FRIEDA: What's he saying?
RITA: You're asking me?
WILL: I'm saying everything that happened then, is happening to us, our generation, again, now. It just goes on. Winners and losers and we're losers.
FRIEDA: He's talking in tongues.
RITA: Why's he do that?
MORG: Talk in tongues?
FRIEDA: Groan. Mutter. Blabber, jabber. All that.
MORG: He hears things. Things we can't hear.
FRIEDA: Hears things that aren't there!
MORG: I said hears things we can't hear, doesn't mean they're not there. He's sensitive to sound.
RITA: Hears things happening a long way off?

MORG: Hears things happening a long time ago.
FRIEDA: Hears the past? Scientifically impossible.
MORG: So we're told but what say sound behaves in ways we haven't learnt to measure? We think sound waves die. What if they don't? What if conversations—
FRIEDA: Conversations.
MORG: Music.
RITA: Music.
MORG: Laughter.
WILL: Laughter.
MORG: Sound of all sorts doesn't decay, doesn't just fade away, what say it builds up in the audio environment?
RITA: Like a kind of pollution?
FRIEDA: You're as mad as he is.
MORG: Am I? Say this place is what—a hundred years old? This place, any place, in a hundred years people deposit a lot of noise, leave a lot of sound behind them. Everything that's happened since these walls have been standing. Everything these walls have been a party to. Births, deaths, marriages, people getting it on with each other. If you could hear all that, if all that history was coming back at you, you'd go mad.
RITA: And he did? Has?
MORG: Wouldn't you?
FRIEDA: Say I buy that idea, if it's there, a hundred years of sound coming back at him, why's it not coming back at us?
MORG: It is, but our ears, our brains, our nervous systems filter it out.
FRIEDA: His don't? So we're looking at a new development in human evolution?
MORG: Or a breakdown in it—your guess is as good as mine.
RITA: My pick is you watched too much television when you were a sprog.
WILL: We don't watch television, television watches us. Like living in an elephant's graveyard, the sound skeletons of the history of television surround us. Pummelling our bodies. Invading our spaces, and our brains. TV eats us out, locks in the 'Brady Bunch', 'Mork and Mindy', 'The Flintstones', 'The Simpsons', seeping into the floor, or the walls, 'Neighbours', sinking into the furniture, 'Ohio Dentists', eating into architecture like a cancer.
MORG: Sound theory's his speciality.

WILL: We're gonna die here, aren't we?
MORG: Time you had a mix, Billy Boy.
WILL: That's why I'm hearing only drak stuff, I'm gonna die here.
RITA: Is that his medication? How often does he take it?
MORG: Not as often as he should.
WILL: This place isn't good for me.
MORG: It'll have to do for now. And these you'll have to take.
FRIEDA: And if he doesn't you'll force him?
MORG: Know another way?
WILL: When you're different they try and break your will, grind you down.
FRIEDA: Authority sucks.
MORG: Come on Will, a green pill and a red or I'll blue on.
FRIEDA: You don't have to hit him!
MORG: You like it, don't you, Will. [*To* FRIEDA] He confuses violence with affection.
FRIEDA: You don't. You're on a power trip right? You're the sort of person who needs an invalid to validate their own existence.
MORG: I'll pretend that's one more thing I didn't hear.
WILL: The sixties.
RITA: Here we go again.
FRIEDA: Medicine you gave him seems to work wonders.
MORG: It will. Will!
FRIEDA: You're a real miracle worker, aren't you?
MORG: If he asks for water don't give him any.
RITA: Got none to give.
MORG: It makes his condition worse.
WILL: The sixties was a time of plenty. Everyone's cup ranneth over. But not in this house. In 1961 it came on the market this place, and thereby hangs a tale.
FRIEDA: Told by an idiot?

SCENE FIVE

Transformation to the sixties begins.

WILL: A couple, keen to buy it, came to inspect the house.

> WILL *plays* ALDISS *and* RITA *plays* TESS, *a couple checking out the house in the 1960s.*

TESS: Aldiss.
ALDISS: What?
TESS: What do you think?
ALDISS: About?
TESS: The floor.
ALDISS: The floor?
TESS: Has it got borer, termites, white ants? Shouldn't we check it for things like that? I love you.
ALDISS: I love you. I don't love borer termites or white ants.
TESS: Any?
ALDISS: None.
TESS: The place is sound. Five thousand five hundred.

> *An auction begins with* MORG *playing* JOHN *and* ROSE *playing* FRIEDA.

JOHN: Five six.
ROSE: Five seven.
JOHN: Stop bidding against me.
ROSE: I wasn't, was I?
JOHN: You were. Five eight.
ROSE: Now you're bidding against me.
ALDISS: Five eight?
TESS: We've got it, haven't we?
ALDISS: Five nine.
TESS: Now we've got it.
JOHN: Five ten.
TESS: We haven't got it.
JOHN: Five ten? I mean six.
ALDISS: Six one.
TESS: Now we'll get it.
ALDISS: Six two.
TESS: Sure to get it.
ALDISS: Six three.
TESS: It's practically ours.
ALDISS: That other couple, they're sticking with us.
TESS: Don't they know this is our dream home?
WILL: 1961.
TESS: Six one.

ALDISS: They already have six three.
JOHN: Twelve.
TESS: We're out of it.
ROSE: Twelve two.
TESS: But we love the house.
ROSE: Twelve three.
ALDISS: Real estate's gone crazy.
TESS: But we love the house.
WILL: The first couple didn't stand a chance.
TESS: We're out of the running.
WILL: The other couple set up house.
ROSE: We'll put the furniture like this.
TESS: Does there always have to be winners and losers?
WILL: There was then. There always will be, that's what I'm saying!
ROSE: And the yellow carpet.
JOHN: With flecks.
ROSE: Wall to wall broadloom. That's what we see.
JOHN: When we come home from work.
ROSE: Carol King's on the radio.
JOHN: We eat our dinner.
ROSE: I love our radio, John.
JOHN: It's not a radio, Rose.
ROSE: It's a Kreisler.
JOHN: Three-in-one.
ROSE: Home.
JOHN: Entertainment unit.
WILL: They're so happy.
ROSE: I love you.
JOHN: I love you.
TESS: They don't count on us turning up.
ROSE: What's that noise?
JOHN: Someone's at the window.
ROSE: She was at the auction.
JOHN: So was he.
ALDISS: Would it be alright if we looked around?
JOHN: She seems—
ALDISS: Disturbed? And why not? Three months ago we'd saved the deposit for a home. I'd opened my own butcher's shop. Things were

going well. Australia, the lucky country.
TESS: Lucky for some.
ALDISS: Our parents had put up what money they could, the finance company the rest, but with the credit squeeze the finance company's gone down the chute.
ROSE: Bust?
ALDISS: Kaput. Taking us with it.
TESS: We've lost everything.
JOHN: I see.
ALDISS: If we'd bought this house at auction we'd have lost it too.
TESS: The carpet. How I wanted it. With yellow flecks. Wall to wall broadloom. The kitchen. Exactly how I wanted it.
ALDISS: Stop it! Stop it! Stop it!
WILL: But it doesn't stop!

Transformation back to the present.

SCENE SIX

WILL *is shaking, in the grip of a fit of some sort.*

WILL: The thirties—the nineties—the sixties—now! Sooner or later everyone living here gets done in! And our crime?!

He sits, suddenly calm.

I'll have a rest.
MORG: Good idea. And while you're doing that I'll check out the rest of this joint.
WILL: I don't need to. I lived here.
MORG: That's right. You already know the building. [*To* RITA] Coming?
RITA: Shouldn't someone—?
MORG: Keep an eye on him, and on the street? She can do that.
FRIEDA: You. Do this. You. Do that. You really are into giving orders, aren't you?
MORG: So you got a better plan?
RITA: [*yelling*] Godsake, if four people can't get it together enough to spend a night in one room what chance is there!

A silence descends. MORG *and* RITA *move away.* FRIEDA *moves, as if on guard, to the window, checking how safe they are.* WILL *lies down and gathers a few rags around him for a bed.*

SCENE SEVEN

A *split scene.* FRIEDA *and* WILL *inside the room*, MORG *and* RITA *outside it in an upper level of the house.*

RITA: I'll write about all this, she said.

MORG: Yeah.

RITA: In my book. I'm writing a book, she said. And she was, writing a book. About all this. She didn't know why. To tell herself when she was scared. Or alone. I'm writing a book, she said.

MORG: This book, how's it begin?

RITA: It begins: everything she stole—and she stole a lot—everything she stole she bartered.

MORG: This she?

RITA: Me.

MORG: Everything she stole.

RITA: She bartered. Sometimes for food. Sometimes for clothes. For medicine. For tools. For seeds. For water.

> *Downstairs,* WILL *is humming melody of 'Over the Hill'.* FRIEDA *is still standing guard.*

MORG: Why seeds?

RITA: She was building a collection of seeds. Wheat seed, barley seed, twenty sorts of lettuce. But you had to know what you were doing. A lot of seed you could get was a trap.

MORG: Lotta new diseases?

RITA: Lotta hybrids. Plants threw seed but it proved infertile.

MORG: Why tools?

RITA: He'd told her they'd need tools.

MORG: He? This he? Who are we talking about?

RITA: She didn't know. She'd only ever heard his voice in dreams. All she knew was he knew things she needed to know. She was waiting for him.

MORG: Mr Right.

RITA: If you like.

MORG: And then she and Mr Right—cos it's a romance—do what?

RITA: Go inland.

MORG: Bushland? Joking. Out there's worse than here.

RITA: Says who?

MORG: The grapevine.
RITA: The grapevine's unreliable.
MORG: Alright, the leaflets they drop, farming's finished.
RITA: She didn't believe the leaflets. They were a scam, she said. To keep people like her from breaking out of the city.
MORG: That's what she wants—to break out of the city?
RITA: That's what she wants.

Downstairs, FRIEDA *yells up to them.*

FRIEDA: You'll tell me if you find anything worth knowing about?.
RITA: Sure. You'll tell us if anything untoward comes down the street?
FRIEDA: Of course.
MORG: [*to* RITA] Will will. He's got good ears. You writing this book with a pen?
RITA: What happened to pens? Pens were obsolete.
MORG: Here's a pen.
RITA: Last time I saw a pen was at school.
MORG: Last time I saw a pen was in gaol.
RITA: Did it work?
MORG: Yeah, as a knife. It got me out of there. They told me I had to pay my debt to society. I said when's society gonna pay its debt to me.

He sticks the pen/knife into the floor. Seeing it used as a weapon focuses her.

RITA: Makes you a character, she says, you'll be in my book.
MORG: This book… ?
RITA: I'm writing it in my head, she says.
MORG: Describing me?
RITA: Two eyes and a nose.
MORG: What are the eyes for?
RITA: You tell me.
MORG: Looking for joy.
RITA: Finding any?
MORG: Finding plenty. What's the nose for?
RITA: It divides the eyes.

Downstairs, FRIEDA *calls to them again.*

FRIEDA: Where are you two?.

RITA: In the bathroom.
MORG: We think there might be some water.
FRIEDA: They've turned the water off.
MORG: In the hot water service.
RITA: Water left in the hot water service.

> FRIEDA *opens* RITA's *rucksack. She withdraws a laptop style device.*

Edward John Eyre, one of the inland explorers we learned about, Edward John Eyre goes fifteen hundred miles, she says, East to West, carrying a boat for godsake, not once does he cross running water.
MORG: History?
RITA: He says.
MORG: I read the Classix Comic. 1787 the First Fleet sails for Australia. One thousand four hundred and seventy three men and women. Makes landfall 1788. Australia Day.
RITA: Soldiers sailors officers quacks.
MORG: Cons and screws, crims and jacks. What's changed? Nothing, cons and screws, just more of us and more of them. When wasn't Australia a penal colony?
RITA: I know that history, she says.
MORG: Seven hundred and seventy-eight convict males, he says.
RITA: One hundred and ninety-two female malcontents, she says.
MORG: You doing a line for me?
RITA: Might be.
MORG: But might not?
RITA: I dunno what I'm doing with my life, she announces, changing the subject. A woman like me—
MORG: Is looking for her next meal, same as the rest of us.
RITA: A woman like me, years ago, I'd be thinking about babies, getting married, setting up house. Normal things.
MORG: Normal things have stopped being normal.
RITA: Do you ever feel like settling down?
MORG: For more than an hour?
RITA: He says.
MORG: No. The times don't allow it.
RITA: Are the times the enemy of love, she asks?
MORG: Have some joy.

RITA: I don't use it. It's addictive. You get skinny—then die. Thought you wanted to check out the rest of the house.
MORG: Out of that room is what I wanted.
RITA: Away from him?
MORG: Him, her, it—the troubles.
RITA: He says. And she watches him preparing to use the drug. I don't use, she says.
MORG: You should.
RITA: He says—
MORG: It helps—
RITA: He says, she says: joy's a designer drug.
MORG: Designed as?
RITA: An appetite suppressant. When they found out what was happening to the food chain they rushed it into production. It's so people like you and me won't know we're slowly being starved to death. It's an appetite suppressant, she says.
MORG: Not all it does. [*Yelling to* FRIEDA] He alright?
WILL: [*whispering*] Sleeping.
FRIEDA: [*yelling back*] Sleeping!

> *Downstairs,* FRIEDA *has found a VR deck in* RITA*'s rucksack and booted it up. Upstairs,* MORG *has cut his arm and fixes a patch of joy on the cut.*

MORG: Rip up the lino while I dismantle the hot water service.
RITA: With what? My bare hands?
MORG: Get her jemmy.
RITA: She's right. You do like giving orders.
MORG: Do I?
RITA: She could see the strain on his face.
MORG: Or am I good at seeing, and saying, what has to be done?
RITA: She was writing a book in her head, she said. She didn't know why. About all this. Everyone has a story. She was writing hers. She didn't know why. Something to tell herself when she was scared. Or alone. A record of the times they found themselves in. Something to leave behind.

> RITA *turns to go for the jemmy. Freezes in the room.* FRIEDA *is keying the VR, still humming.* WILL *has got out of bed. Watching* FRIEDA, *he circles. He stops humming.*

WILL: I keep hearing voices.
FRIEDA: Saying?
WILL: Telling me to kill you.
FRIEDA: People been trying to kill me for years.
WILL: I'm gonna use a brick, when you're sleeping, bring a brick down on your head.
FRIEDA: That's a good plan.
WILL: I know.
FRIEDA: One problem.
WILL: I haven't got a brick?
FRIEDA: I don't sleep.
WILL: If I sleep I wake up smelling that smell.
FRIEDA: What smell's that?
WILL: Fried nerve ends. Burnt out synapses. My own.
FRIEDA: You don't have to shut the door.
WILL: We might do sex, or haven't you got time?
FRIEDA: Residia's what I've got.

That news changes WILL*'s intent.*

What did happen to romance?
WILL: It didn't survive the thirties.
FRIEDA: People still use the word: ro-mance.
WILL: Didn't get past the bomb. Hiroshima and Nagasaki. 1945 is year one in my calendar.
FRIEDA: People still think romantic thoughts.
WILL: AIDS and Residia have put romance off the agenda.
FRIEDA: They did put you away, didn't they?
WILL: Oh yes. You wouldn't believe the things I've seen, the things that have happened to me.
FRIEDA: Anything bad happens to me I erase it from my memory. Erase. Wipe. Delete.
WILL: No editorial function's my problem. I'm full time retrieval and storage. No delete key, see. Woke up one morning knowing too much. It drove me to suicide.
FRIEDA: Suicide didn't work?
WILL: Obviously suicide didn't work! It didn't work six times! I even used electricity—even it failed. Hanging, that I haven't tried. I could rip up these rags, make a rope, a noose, a loop.

He's lain down again. RITA *enters.*

RITA: You got that going, she said.

FRIEDA: I ratted your rucksack. I'm having a play. A Laserex K-Tel Somatic. Where'd you come by a machine like this?

RITA: Stole it. Mob I was with scragged an Electro-Mart.

FRIEDA: This is the Ferrari of Virtuals.

RITA: You fly with electronics? A nerd bird?

FRIEDA: If I was some gang'd have me, I'd be useful.

RITA: The gangs don't take women.

FRIEDA: I've heard there's a gang of cyber chicks.

RITA: And?

FRIEDA: I'm for checking out a rumour like that.

WILL: I'm planning my next suicide attempt.

RITA: Good, we're all busy then. He wants me to rip up the lino. Can I use your jemmy, she says?

FRIEDA: If you get me his memory stick.

RITA: Has he got one?

FRIEDA: Pinned to his top-pocket.

RITA takes the jemmy and moves towards WILL.

WILL: No.

RITA: Why not? She needs it.

WILL: It's got my CV on it.

RITA: Your CV! Your bloody CV!

FRIEDA: Quickly, before this crashes.

RITA: You're unemployable. We're all unemployable. She didn't know why she was angry.

He hands her the memory stick.

But she was. She didn't want to be angry, but couldn't help herself.

She hands FRIEDA *the memory stick.* FRIEDA *slots it.*

RITA: There's a glove goes with that.

FRIEDA: Don't need it. I jacked in with my own set of cephs. Digital motion capture.

She indicates encephalograph patches attached to her forearms and neck.

RITA: You need goggles too I'm told but I lost em.

FRIEDA: I have my own.

> FRIEDA *dons goggles.* RITA *returns upstairs.*

RITA: No water, she asked, back in the bathroom, looking up.
MORG: Header tank's empty.
RITA: He'd climbed into the roof.
MORG: But the main tank sounds promising.
RITA: Let's hope so, she says. She could hear him working somewhere above her.

> *She kneels to rip up the lino.* MORG *continues working in the roof. Below VR deck running how she wants,* FRIEDA *begins a dance programming patterns into it.* WILL *sits in a yoga pose.*

WILL: Schizophrenia is caused by the fact that young people no longer obey their parents. *Journal of Mental Science,* 1904.
FRIEDA: The science of mental health has a dubious record.
WILL: Tell me about it.
FRIEDA: A lot of science has a dubious record but without it we'd still be in the dark ages.
WILL: We are in the dark ages.
FRIEDA: Are we? Why's that?
WILL: Because human beings are sacks of pus. Torn condoms crammed with venom. Sheathes of hate.
FRIEDA: If we're that bad why'd we get up off all fours?
WILL: To more efficiently massacre everyone and everything around us.
FRIEDA: Is that the best you can do?
WILL: Human beings are a virus.
FRIEDA: What's our function?
WILL: To give the planet influenza—smarten up.
FRIEDA: That's drak talk. It brings me down.
WILL: That's the function of drak talk.
FRIEDA: To bring me down?
WILL: To smarten you up.
FRIEDA: If I said I feel sorry for you—
WILL: I'd say pity's a pathetic emotion. Can you do something real for me instead?
FRIEDA: Can a virus invent a virus, and project it?

RITA: Why do I rip up this lino?
MORG: You'll be able to tell if the flooring's been messed with. Could be whoever lived here's hidden some food.
WILL: What do you think, really think, about the times, about what's going on out there?
FRIEDA: I've heard it's the last days of Rome, but there'll be survivors, and elsewhere the living will get on with the business of living.
WILL: File that under R.
FRIEDA: R for what?
WILL: R for ridiculous rumours.
FRIEDA: You don't think this is a re-run, a repeat?
WILL: I think this is new.
FRIEDA: And it's the end?
WILL: And it's the end. Name another species that tries to kill its young.
FRIEDA: Some do, when threatened.
WILL: Greed protects greed, that's what this is all about. The old hanging onto the old world whatever the cost. The insane perpetuating their insanity.

> *Chaser lights pulse on* FRIEDA*'s goggles. He stands—to check what she's doing.*

Somebody says to Gandhi: how long before India has a standard of living like Britain's? And Gandhi says: Britain's a small country, but to secure that standard of living for itself it had to conquer half the world. India's a big country. How many worlds are there?
FRIEDA: More worlds than Gandhi dreamed possible.
WILL: But not enough to save the day. Greed wins. End of game.

> *He is staring at the VR as she dances.*

WILL: I'm going to die in this house.
FRIEDA: You don't know that.
WILL: I think that. I think the sweepers will come crabbing down that street and blast us to bits.
FRIEDA: What if we blast them back.
WILL: With what?
FRIEDA: With this.
WILL: A virtual? It's a toy.
FRIEDA: Not a toy. Top of the range. A Laserex K-tel Somatic.

WILL: Then it's a rich man's toy. Virtuals. When reality got so drak they started making virtuals.

He is removing his shoes and some clothing, making a mound in his bed as though it is him.

Deprived of the ability to control the real world, sell people the means of controlling inner space, and in selling that, invade the human sensorium totally.

FRIEDA: Virtual Reality. The last frontier.

WILL: Well, nobody controls my inner space.

FRIEDA: Maybe that's what they found out. How uncontrollable people's inner space is. Why do you think they wanted machines like this taken off the market?

WILL: Cost of components.

FRIEDA: Cost of letting them fall into the wrong hands.

WILL: That's a rumour.

FRIEDA: But you've heard it.

WILL: I hear a lot of things.

FRIEDA: I've noticed. The oomph of the 'made in India' chips in these things had Motorola and Intel shitting bricks. Turns out they're more powerful than anyone suspected.

Intercut RITA *and* MORG.

RITA: Ever seen stars?

MORG: Gonna do me a favour and knock me out?

RITA: I thought I already had, she said. I mean real stars.

MORG: Yeah, I grew up on a diet of MTV and Rage.

RITA: I mean up there. The sky. Ever looked at the sky?

MORG: Too much UV.

RITA: She's joined him in the roof. Can see out across the city through a hole where the tiles are smashed, missing. Ever trod on a bug?

MORG: Is that an accusation?

RITA: An enquiry—a cockroach—ever trod on a cockroach? Ever tortured an ant? So much life even in something that small. How can Nature be dying?

MORG: Who knows, but it is.

RITA: She's joined him in the roof.

MORG: No water up here. Any food down there?

RITA: No food, she says. And they look out through a hole in the tiles, through a break in the pollution, past the drifts of sulphur. Into the interstellar depths.
MORG: Mars. Where the temperatures are three thousand degrees centigrade. Venus where no organism stirs in the frozen wastes.
RITA: The vast immensity of nature doesn't impress you?
MORG: Nature fought us—
RITA: He tells me—
MORG: And lost, I should know.
RITA: How?
MORG: Do I know? Cos I grew up in the country, little girl.
RITA: She didn't like 'little'. Probably didn't like 'girl'. But let it pass.
MORG: Cos one day I woke up and all our cows were dead. And three days later, all our pigs had followed suit. And the day after that, the old man shot himself. And two days later the old lady took off with the people next door. Only room in the car for one of you, I hear 'em saying. And only enough petrol to get to Albury anyway. Better a long shot than no shot at all. My mum's plastered on sherry.
RITA: Albury was bombed.
MORG: I know. Bye bye Mum.
RITA: I still believe in the power of nature, she says. I think we can get back to the way we were.
MORG: How quaint.

Below, WILL *is inspecting the VR's screen.*

WILL: What's all this crap?
FRIEDA: I've walked in a grid of the city.
WILL: The red moving bits?
FRIEDA: Sweepers.
WILL: And we're where?
FRIEDA: X marks the spot.
WILL: So they're headed our way.
FRIEDA: They may be headed our way. That's an option they've got. They're doing a prelim on the neighbourhood.
WILL: This is in real time?
FRIEDA: Checking the cost benefit options. I'm reading their minds.
MORG: By virtualling? It can't be done.
FRIEDA: By modeling the options. Can be done. And I just did it.

WILL: Big electrical fire out there. I'm receiving the static.
FRIEDA: So's my screen. They've taken out the old telephone exchange.

Intercuts from roof to room.

RITA: Big fire.
MORG: Where?
RITA: Out there.
MORG: They're choking escape routes. The 'she' in your book, she wants out of the city?
RITA: That's what 'she' wants.
WILL: You're plugged into Army HQ? Don't worry, your secret's safe with me.
FRIEDA: Nothing's safe with you. But yes. That bit of flex. It's a fibre-optics cable linking me to High Command.
WILL: High Command? High's what I should be thinking. I need that bit of flex.
FRIEDA: I was joking so be my guest.
WILL: You're off your head right? A dumb chick making like she's a hacker.
FRIEDA: A cyber freak. Hanging by the thread of my own sanity.
WILL: Join the club.
FRIEDA: Thank you. I've plotted a scenario using the probabilities I know about from being on the streets today. I've factored in number of vehicles, size of forces I saw. I'm onto every move they're likely to make.
WILL: You're madder than I am.
FRIEDA: The options are West, the pirate radio station, or East for random kills, targeting, for example, houses.
WILL: Houses?
FRIEDA: Dumpsters.
WILL: Dumpsters?
FRIEDA: Doorways. Dead ends. Nooks crannies hidey-holes.
WILL: East? Here is East. Why won't they go North?
FRIEDA: Why bother? North is uncontested ground. They laid waste to it days ago. The Hippy Gardens.
WILL: I ate there once. Dined like a king.

He has ripped some flex from the wall, made it into a tie. She continues to dance.

MORG: And the 'he' in your book? He's from the country?
RITA: And wants to get back to it.
FRIEDA: East it is. They're moving east.
WILL: It's 1897. I'm going to work. In 1897 even tradesmen wear ties.
RITA: Will was right about this house. In 1961 the place was on the market. I found an old newspaper under the lino she tells him. All I found.
WILL: In 1897 a person my age died here. The person my age was out of work. House was half built. Begun height of the land boom, the 1890s Depression brought construction to a halt.

    WILL *is back in the 1890s.*

RITA: [*reading from newspaper clipping*] 'Spacious older style brick home in sought after area. Only minutes to shops and station. Features three bedrooms, lounge with marble fireplace. Separate dining room. Large verandah. This home has been neglected.'
WILL: Half-built it had been left exposed to the weather.
RITA: 'But boasts lots of character and period detail. Ideal for restoration. Well worth inspection.' This address. See, the ad's been circled.
FRIEDA: They'll encircle the suburb.
RITA: Will wasn't making it up. This house was put up for sale, August 1961, he does hear things!
MORG: He'll hear the sweepers before they come through.
FRIEDA: They'll come through a street at a time.
MORG: Why I hang with him. He's a walking early warning system.
RITA: Saved your hide, has he?
MORG: Got me hiding when I wasn't gonna.
WILL: This person my age, years out of work, thinks 'Apprentice'? I'll take it. Sounds the go. Signs on. A skinflint builder's agreed to restart the build. Sweats everyone he hires. Pays way below the going rate. People take it. Where there's misery there's dollars to be made.
MORG: Should we join the others?
FRIEDA: Wake me when they get here.
WILL: The others?
FRIEDA: The sweepers you durh.

    FRIEDA *rests up for the task ahead.*

RITA: Soon enough will be soon enough.

She and MORG *kiss.*

WILL: It's 1897. I'm weak with hunger but glad to be starting a job. What I don't know is rain, damp, long exposure to the elements has weakened the footings. The building's front section is about to collapse. On me.

WILL *has mounted scaffolding.*

MORG *and* RITA *return, seeing* FRIEDA *first.*

MORG: Catching some zeds? How's he been?
FRIEDA: The better for you not being here.
WILL: If at first you don't succeed.

MORG *and* RITA *see* WILL *on high.*

FRIEDA: Your re-arrival seems to have triggered a relapse.
MORG: Thanks for keeping an eye on him.
FRIEDA: I've been keeping an eye on other things.
WILL: It's 1897 and I'm perched amidst the upper levels, looking towards my far horizons.
MORG: Do it. Jump. See if I care.
FRIEDA: It's his seventh suicide attempt.

WILL *leaps, holding flex tie as a rope.*

WILL: I must be a cat.
FRIEDA: He's engaged, yet again, in attention-seeking behaviour.
WILL: I must have nine goddam lives!
FRIEDA: Best interpreted as a cry for help, but one we can't attend. Help being something we ourselves are just as much in need of.
MORG: We're going.
WILL: Good idea. This house and that woman are driving me nuts.
MORG: [*indicating* RITA] She and me are going.
WILL: I start to see a problem.
RITA: What's the problem?
WILL: You're the problem, baby.
MORG: You're welcome to come with us.
RITA: Am I still the problem?
MORG: She's got some seeds and tools to pick up. We're gonna try and break through the cordon. Go bush. You in or out?
FRIEDA: Me?

WILL: Me?
FRIEDA: Start a kibbutz?
WILL: Start a kibbutz?
FRIEDA: Re-invent the Garden of Eden?
WILL: Re-invent the Garden of Eden?
FRIEDA: Live happily ever after?
WILL: Live happily ever after?
FRIEDA: Not my style.
WILL: Not my style.
FRIEDA: I'm asphalt and concrete.
WILL: I'm asphalt and concrete.
FRIEDA: The only animals I know are—
WILL: Zebra crossings.
FRIEDA: Zebra crossings.
MORG: Don't say you weren't given a chance.
FRIEDA: I wish I had a chance.
WILL: She's got Residia.
FRIEDA: I've been given something else.
MORG: I'm sorry to hear that.
FRIEDA: Not half as sorry as I was, given the news. Fancy using rapists as vectors to wage chemical and biological warfare against all women under twenty-five. Relapse. Prolapse. Collapse.
RITA: I'd like you to come with us.
FRIEDA: I said I pass. If you're going get going cos they're coming.
MORG: Who is?
FRIEDA: Sweepers are. Correction. One sweeper.
MORG: Will?
WILL: Can't hear a thing. My brain's full of snakes, lizards, insects.
RITA: Living things. That's a good sign.
WILL: Sure, would be if we weren't on the list.
RITA: Of?
WILL: Of endangered living things.

  WILL, RITA and MORG exit. FRIEDA stays with the VR.

RITA: What happened was this:
MORG: We cleared the building, reached some waste ground, paused to look back.
RITA: The sweeper had stopped. Frieda had stayed behind.

WILL: It's sensing her.
RITA: The flash as the sweeper let off a laser trace. It sliced through the building, brought the house down.

In slow motion the window collapses.

MORG: Through the rubble and dust we saw her. One hand still going like crazy. The other clutching the VR to her chest.
RITA: It was Will who moved first.
MORG: He knew before we did.
RITA: Knew before she did.
MORG: We were waiting for a second blast.
RITA: So was she.
MORG: It never came.
WILL: [*to* FRIEDA] You souped it!
FRIEDA: I souped it?
WILL: Good static.
FRIEDA: Electronic smear. Wipe. Circuits to confetti. Wipe.
WILL: White noise.
MORG: She's pale.
WILL: Wouldn't you be? Half her being must have gone into that.
RITA: How hurt?
MORG: Bleeding. Not badly.
WILL: Can you believe it—she souped a sweeper!
MORG: Clock the smile.

They support the dazed FRIEDA.

RITA: And why not the smile? She had held in her hand the rock David used against Goliath.

Show ends with 'Over the Hill' acapella.

SONG: On the other side of the hill,
The sun is always shining,
On the other side of the hill,
There'll be an end to pining,
When we stand on the top of the hill,
If we've been givers not takers,
We'll see the golden acres,
On the other side of the hill.
RITA: More sweepers were already on their way. But we'd be gone,

carrying her, and it, that VR model, across waste ground, through drifts of sulphur and stench, a steel dawn breaking, but a song in our hearts. Will's mad song of a golden age, a song people have always sung in all the languages that have ever been.

FRIEDA: From COBOL to Java to… Nouveau Bach?

SONG: Though the stormy clouds are o'er us,
    Somewhere the blue birds fly,
    If we keep on straight before us,
    We'll find them by and bye,
    Till we get right over the hill,
    We're only poor beginners,
    But maybe we'll be winners,
    On the other side of the hill.

THE END

The Bridge
Chris Thompson

Photo: Susan Gordon-Brown

CHRIS THOMPSON is a writer, artistic director, arts educator and arts consultant. A writer for more than twenty years, Chris works in film, theatre and television. He has won two AWGIE awards for his plays, *Shady Characters* and *The Bridge* and received nominations for *A Neutral Script* and *Spinning the Line*. He has also had a number of short stories published in anthologies for young adult readers including *If You Sleep You Die* which won the 1992 Nillumbik Alan Marshall award. His feature film work includes *Jigsaw* (Colosimo Films, 1989) and *A Slow Night at the Kuwaiti Café* (Boulevard Films, 1991).

Michael Wahr as Aaron in the 2008 La Mama production. (Photo: Susan Gordon-Brown)

The Bridge was first performed by HotHouse Theatre at The Butter Factory Theatre, Albury-Wodonga, on 26 April 2002, with the following cast:

AARON	Simon Stone
DESLEY	Sharyn Oppy
REG/MISTER DONNEL	Ken Radley
RITA	Victoria Eagger
BUSHY/RUDY	Matthew Green

Director, Wayne Hope
Designer, Leon Salom
Composer, Craig Pilkington
Lighting Designer, Rob Scott

The Bridge was comissioned by HotHouse Theatre, and was developed with the assistance of creative development workshop material from Margot Fenley, Wayne Hope and Rob Lyon as well as Jane Bayly and Tom Considine, with Kirsten von Bibra (director/dramaturg) and Naomi Edwards (YPAA Mentor Project), Kylie Fahey (Greater Murray Health Service), Wiggy Brennan (HotHouse Theatre Artistic Directorate) and Sue Riddell (HotHouse Theatre Community Liaison) and with dramaturgical assistance from Wayne Hope and Maude Davey. Its creative development was funded by The Ian Potter Foundation, The William Buckland Foundation and The R.E. Ross Trust.

The Bridge received its Melbourne at La Mama Theatre on 22 May 2008. The remounted season was produced by randomACTS and directed by Chris Thompson. It was performed by Michael Wahr, Caity Fowler, Kurt Geyer, Margot Fenley and Martin Croft, with lighting by Danny Pettingill, design by the company and music by Caity Fowler.

CHARACTERS

AARON
REG
RITA
DESLEY
BUSHY
MR DONNEL
GILLIAN
DONNY (recorded voice)
REG and MR DONNEL can be doubled
DESLEY and GILLIAN can be doubled

SETTING

In the space is the bridge… an abandoned wooden bridge spanning a country railway line. Within the play other places are created with furniture and light. Act One takes place the week that Donny died. Act Two takes place the week of the deb ball.

ACT ONE

SCENE ONE

Monday afternoon.

The sound of a diesel train in the distance.

AARON *in his room, isolated in light, playing his bass guitar.*

He plays a driving, angry riff over and over again.

The sound of a diesel train… coming closer…

The pitch of the diesel's horn shifts; the Doppler effect as it passes beneath the bridge.

A sound like a falling cry.

AARON *breaks a string on his guitar.*

AARON: Fuck!

> *The scene opens up to the family kitchen.*
>
> REG *has commandeered the kitchen table, tinkering with a greasy carburettor, laid out on newspaper. His crossing guard uniform and sign are hanging nearby.*
>
> RITA *is perched, awkwardly, working out something in her diary.*
>
> *They're in the middle of a conversation.*

REG: It's all talk, this town. Always has been, always will be. They're never gonna close that bridge.

RITA: The boy's dead, Reg. [*The carburettor is too much for her.*] Do you have to do this here?

REG: I put paper down.

RITA: I've got to finish this.

REG: I've got some news.

> RITA *is concentrating on what she's doing.* REG *waits. She tries to show interest.*

Allan's offered me a couple'a days work blowing out a new dam. Pick up the gelignite, help him set the charges, that sort of thing.

Not much money, but it'll help. [*Beat.*] It'll be good to be working again.

AARON comes into the room, an empty Coke bottle in his hand.

AARON: We got any more Coke?

RITA: Sorry, I meant to go on the way home.

AARON: That'd be a no.

He throws the bottle in the bin.

RITA: We were just talking about... you know, the... that... that poor boy...

AARON: Donny. His name's Donny.

RITA: Donny. [*She struggles, checks her watch.*] How did the other kids take it? It's been such a hectic day, I hardly had a moment to... You know, if you want to talk you only have to...

AARON: There's nothing to drink.

RITA: There's no shame in feeling...

AARON: How would you know what I'm feeling?

RITA: That's why I... if you'd like to...

AARON's suddenly too close to RITA.

AARON: Okay. Let's talk. Right now.

RITA: [*taken by surprise*] Sure. As soon as I get home. I promise.

AARON: Forget it. Can I have twenty bucks?

RITA: What do you need money for?

AARON: I broke a guitar string.

RITA: I thought you got paid after Saturday?

He cuts her dead, turns to REG.

AARON: Dad?

REG: What?

AARON: Can you lend it to me?

RITA: I didn't say I wouldn't lend it to you.

REG: What?

AARON: Can I borrow twenty bucks?

REG: Have you asked your mother?

RITA: I don't think I have that much on me.

AARON is frustrated with everything and needs an outlet. It might as well be his dad.

AARON: What are you doin' with that? You're not on the farm anymore, Dad. You're a Lollipop Man. Take it down the servo like normal people.
REG: [*a look*] We're called Crossing Supervisors.

    REG *gathers his things together, leaves.*

AARON: [*to* RITA] Can I borrow it or not?
RITA: You'd have to take my card.
AARON: Forget it. If it's such a big deal, I'll lend it off Des.

    AARON *leaves.*

RITA: [*calling after him*] I didn't say I wouldn't lend it to you!

    She waits but there's no response.

[*Calling*] What about dinner?!

    He's gone.

Shit! [*She checks her watch.*] Shit!

    RITA *leaves.*

SCENE TWO

Wednesday afternoon.

AARON *is up at the bridge. He has climbed up onto its structure, restless and manic, clowning around, testing his limits.*

DESLEY *enters. She stands at the edge, looking over, looking down.*

This is where it happened.

AARON *drops down behind her, grabs her.*

AARON: Watch it, Des.
DESLEY: [*startled*] Fuck, Aaron. You scared the shit out of me.

    AARON *grins and climbs back up, monkeying around above her head.*

What are you doing?
AARON: You ever get that feeling? Like you're up really high and you feel like you're gonna jump. Like you have to, just to see what would happen? [*His balance wavers.*] Whoa…
DESLEY: Aaron!
AARON: [*laughing at her*] It's a long way down, Des.

DESLEY: It's not funny, Aaron.
AARON: Jeez, lighten up.

> *He pulls out a marker, starts writing on the wood.*

DESLEY: Now what are you doing?
AARON: [*stirring her up*] Desley was here.
DESLEY: Don't be a dick, Aaron.
AARON: [*mocking*] Don't be a dick, Desley.

> *She moves away.*

Hey, I'm not the only one. There's heaps of old graffiti and shit up here. Look… 'R and R—fourteenth of February, 1977'. Valentines Day. I wasn't even born.
DESLEY: Some lovesick woos.
AARON: I think it's romantic.

> *He climbs down, plays up to her. She shrugs him off.*

I know. 'Don't be a dick, Aaron.'

> *He moves away, looks off into the distance. The light shifts in the trees.*

Donny would've liked this.
DESLEY: What?
AARON: This. The light in the trees. It's good light.
DESLEY: [*doesn't understand*] It's just sunlight.
AARON: Donny would've liked it. He was into that sort of shit. [*He pulls a bag of dope out of his pocket.*] He was into all sorts of shit.
DESLEY: Where'd you get that?
AARON: I was holding it for Donny.

> *He rolls a joint.* DESLEY *ignores him. He lights up.*

You reckon a bridge is still a bridge if no-one uses it anymore?

> DESLEY *isn't impressed.*

I guess Donny found a use for it.
DESLEY: Don't, alright.
AARON: Don't what?
DESLEY: Just don't.

> *He offers some to* DESLEY. *She shakes her head. He sits. Beat.*

AARON: Haven't seen you for a couple of days.

DESLEY: Keeping busy, you know.
AARON: That's the way, Des. Busy, busy, busy. Just like everyone else.
DESLEY: What's up your arse, Aaron?
AARON: Sorry. I've been a bit weird. Haven't been sleeping. I was gonna ring you last night, only it was about three a.m. Watched the home shopping show and the sex ads instead.
DESLEY: Buy anything good?

He does some muscle-man posing.

AARON: An Abba-Dabba-Doer. What d'you think?
DESLEY: Can you still get your money back?

They laugh together. A more comfortable moment.

You could've called me.
AARON: Call me. Call me now.
DESLEY: I mean it. Any time.
AARON: Yeah. I know.
DESLEY: What'd you want to talk about?
AARON: Stuff. Bullshit. You know.
DESLEY: Donny.

AARON is silent. DESLEY moves closer to him. They embrace for a few moments, then DESLEY feels awkward, pulls away.

AARON: What?
DESLEY: Nothing.
AARON: Hey, I wasn't...
DESLEY: I know.

AARON moves away to the edge of the bridge. Beat.

You're still doing it, aren't you? The deb?
AARON: I said I would, didn't I?
DESLEY: I know, I just... didn't know... you know...
AARON: Life goes on, isn't that what everyone says?

DESLEY watches him for a bit.

DESLEY: It's not disrespectful.
AARON: What?
DESLEY: Doing stuff. Things you enjoy.
AARON: You think I'm gonna enjoy getting dressed up in a dork suit and dancing around the bloody school gym with you?

DESLEY *looks hurt.*
[*Serious*] Joking, Des.
She breaks out in a smile, mocking him.
DESLEY: [*laughing*] Joking, Aaron.
AARON: [*laughing back*] You're so full of shit.
They're easy with each other again.
Whatcha gonna wear?
DESLEY: Like there's a choice.
AARON: No way. The big white dress?
DESLEY: It's a deb ball, Aaron. It's what you wear.
AARON: Yeah, I know. I just thought…
DESLEY: You don't think I'll look any good.
AARON: No. I mean yes. I mean…
DESLEY: You think I'll look fat.
AARON: That's not… I didn't say that.
DESLEY: I will. I'll look like a big meringue.
AARON: [*teasing*] You'll look good. You'll look like a princess.
DESLEY: Yeah. Princess Meringue.

He mock-dances with her. They laugh together.

AARON: Why are you doin' it, if you think it sucks so much?
DESLEY: I didn't say it sucks. It doesn't suck. Not all of it. Just some of it.
AARON: Like the dancing. And the bit with the big white dress.
DESLEY: Not the dancing.
AARON: Why are you doin' it, Des?

She shrugs.

Well, I'm only doin' it 'cos you're doin' it, and if you don't know why you're doing it then why the fuck am I doin' it?

DESLEY *gives him a look like he's trying to back out.*
I said I'm doin' it.

A look from DESLEY.
I'm doing it. Okay?

She runs off. He chases after her.

SCENE THREE

Wednesday afternoon.

BUSHY *and* RITA *come into the staff room.*

RITA: If it's not about food or money he hardly says a word to me.
BUSHY: Pretty typical for a teenage boy.
RITA: Not for Aaron it's not.
BUSHY: Oh. He's special.

>*Their conversation is interrupted by* MR DONNEL *walking through.*

MR DONNEL: So, young Donny caught the five-forty express, eh?
BUSHY: Not funny, Clive.
MR DONNEL: Am I laughing? As far as I'm concerned, it couldn't've happened to a nicer kid. The little shit got what he deserved.

>RITA *might hit him. Instead, she holds out a piece of paper.*

That the slip for my geography excursion?
RITA: New roster.
MR DONNEL: What about my geography excursion?
RITA: We've had other priorities this week.
MR DONNEL: [*looking at the roster*] Oh, bullshit. Yard duty and extra classes to cover for the slackers who can't hack the workload.

>MR DONNEL *leaves.*

BUSHY: Have a nice day, Clive.

>*They watch him go.*

[*To* RITA] You should talk to Desley.

>*She shakes her head.*

If he's talking to anyone, he's talking to her.
RITA: She's a student, Bushy.
BUSHY: She's his friend.
RITA: You talk to her.
BUSHY: Rita.

>*Beat.*

RITA: I know what you're thinking. [*Beat.*] But it's different than when we were kids. I don't like what goes on up there.

BUSHY: And you know what that is?
RITA: I've got a good imagination. They all think it's cool. Who knows what sort of influence kids like Donny are having on them.
BUSHY: What? On kids like Aaron and Desley? Maybe they influenced him.
RITA: Grow up, Bushy. You're not helping.
BUSHY: If Donny had got drunk and smashed himself up in a stolen car you'd be wanting to change the laws and increase the police force. The bridge is the same now as it was when we were kids. The problem was Donny.
RITA: That's bullshit.

> REG *is suddenly standing in the room.*
>
> *He's wearing a t-shirt and leather motorcycle jacket. He's much younger, more alive, more energetic. He's as he was twenty-four years ago. It takes* RITA *by surprise. She's caught somewhere between her memory and the present.*

YOUNG REG: It's not bullshit, Reet.

> *She's confused by his presence.*

It's not. I'm deadset. I'm really going.

> BUSHY *continues, oblivious to* YOUNG REG.

BUSHY: You telling me you never went up there to get drunk and have sex?
RITA: Bushy!
YOUNG REG: Reet!
BUSHY: You can tell me.
YOUNG REG: You know you want to, Reet.
BUSHY: Come on, Rita. A boy like Reg. On that motorbike.
YOUNG REG: You in that blue dress, arms tight around my waist.
BUSHY: Tell the truth.
YOUNG REG: Tell the truth, Reet.
RITA: [*to* REG] No.
BUSHY: Well, I did. Plenty of times.
RITA: Who with?
BUSHY: None of your business.
YOUNG REG: None of your business.
RITA: [*still confused*] What?

YOUNG REG: Where I'm going. It's none of your business…

    YOUNG REG *offers her his hand.*

… unless you want it to be. [*Beat.*] Well?

    RITA *is inside her memory. She takes his hand, steps up onto the bridge. They kiss.*

    Sound of a diesel train in the distance.

Feet or freight?

RITA: What?

YOUNG REG: Feet or freight? Passenger train or goods train?

RITA: Passenger. Just leaving the station. Be here in five minutes.

YOUNG REG: Where do you think they're all going?

RITA: This time of day? It'll be the five-forty express.

YOUNG REG: Yeah, but just imagine. They could be going anywhere. Just like you and me.

RITA: Except we're not going anywhere, and I know it's the five-forty.

YOUNG REG: That teachers college is turning you into a walking timetable.

RITA: Some of us have [*older again*] responsibilities.

BUSHY: You can't be responsible for everyone, Rita. At some point you have to let 'em make up their own minds.

YOUNG REG: I've got responsibilities. The old man's getting on. Pretty soon that farm'll be mine.

RITA: You're going away to God knows where…

YOUNG REG: You've got a live a bit before you die, Reet. Come with me. When we get back you can finish teacher's college and I'll settle down on the farm.

RITA: It's a nice idea, Reggie.

YOUNG REG: Then you'll come?

RITA: I can't, Reggie.

YOUNG REG: [*disappointed*] Oh.

RITA: You go. You should. Sow your wild oats.

    REG *comes over and kisses her.*

YOUNG REG: You're my only wild oat, Reet.

    He pulls out a pocketknife and climbs up onto the bridge.

RITA: Reggie.

YOUNG REG: You know what day it is?
RITA: What are you doing?
YOUNG REG: Come up and see.
RITA: What if we fall?
YOUNG REG: What if we don't?
RITA: Come down.

He carves something into the timber.

YOUNG REG: R and R—Reggie and Reet. Fourteenth of February, 1977. Come on, Reet.
RITA: [*older again*] I'm not going up there.
BUSHY: Maybe you should. Go up there and see for yourself. Get Aaron to take you. It might even get him talking.
RITA: You always know what's best, don't you, Bushy?
BUSHY: Just trying to help.
RITA: I don't want to think about this stuff.

REG climbs down.

YOUNG REG: Think about it, Reet. I've got big plans. The old man's done okay, but he's behind the times. The government's subsidising small dairy farms like ours. A smart guy could make a lot money. A lot of money. I reckon we'll be on a winner.
RITA: We?
YOUNG REG: Me… an' my ol' man.
RITA: Oh.
YOUNG REG: Unless someone else comes along.

He leans in and kisses her.

BUSHY: You don't want to lose him, Rita.
RITA: [*confused, caught between two realities*] What?

REG moves away. RITA is alone with her memory.

BUSHY: Aaron. He's a good kid. You don't want to lose him.

The echo of her memory… then it's back to work.

RITA: If I want advice on how to run my family, I'd hardly ask a middle-aged single man who's never even been married.
BUSHY: [*hurt by the comment*] Sure. You're probably right. Anyway, I've got things to do too.

BUSHY leaves. RITA watches him go.

SCENE FOUR

Wednesday night.

AARON *is on the bridge. He takes a video camera from his bag, flips out the little screen, watches the images. Two voices can be heard. One is* AARON. *The other is* DONNY.

DONNY: Hey, check this out, man.
AARON: Where'd you get that?
DONNY: It's mine. I'm gonna make a movie. Wanna be in it?
AARON: Where'd you get it, Donny?
DONNY: I borrowed it. Fuck, you're as bad as your old lady.
AARON: Is it on? Don't point it at me.
DONNY: Don't shit yourself. Do something.
AARON: What d'you want me to do?
DONNY: I dunno.
AARON: Aren't you the director?
DONNY: Okay. Action.
AARON: You dickhead.

They laugh together for a bit.

Can I have a go?
DONNY: No way, man. Like you said, I'm the fuckin' director.
AARON: Okay, then. I'll do the music.
DONNY: Hey, that'd be awesome.
AARON: Yeah, sure.
DONNY: No, really. I mean it. We should absolutely do that.
AARON: Yeah. Okay.

The sound of a diesel train quite close.

DONNY: Hey, hold onto me, I'll get an action shot of the train.
AARON: Get down, you fuckwit. You'll fall.
DONNY: Yeah, no such luck.

The Doppler effect as the train passes.

AARON: Fuck. [*Beat.*] Donny?

Silence… then…

DONNY: Don't shit yourself, Aaron.
AARON: Why's that little light flashing like that?

DONNY: Oh fuck, it's still on.

They crack up. They might be stoned. Whatever the reason, they're having a good time.

AARON: You're serious about this movie shit, aren't you?

DONNY: I gotta do something to get me outta this shithole. It'd be great. Making up the stories. Figuring out the camera shots. Meeting all those hot movie chicks. Go on, do something.

AARON: You gotta script?

DONNY: Yeah, like I'm gonna write a script. Just riff it. Tell us some hot shit about Des.

AARON: There's nothin' to tell, man.

DONNY: She got nice tits?

AARON: We're just friends, Donny.

DONNY: Bullshit. You want her. You could have her. She'd be easy.

AARON: I told you, man. I don't want to talk about Des.

DONNY: We should get her up here. Do a porno.

AARON: Shut up, Donny. [*Beat.*] What are you doing?

DONNY: You should see this shot, man. The light comin' through this tree. Fuckin' magic.

    AARON *switches it off. Music continues.*

SCENE FIVE

Thursday morning.

AARON *is in Bushy's office, alone. Agitated.*

Suddenly BUSHY *enters.*

BUSHY: How now, thou cream fac'd loon! Where got'st thou that goose look?

    AARON *is totally perplexed.*

AARON: Am I in trouble for something?

    BUSHY *slams a long thin wooden box down on the desk.*

BUSHY: Not with me you're not.

    AARON *looks at the box on the desk.*

Things okay?

AARON: I guess.

BUSHY: Everything alright at home?

　　AARON *gets to his feet.*

AARON: Did my mum tell you to do this?
BUSHY: I just thought we might have a man-to-man. I don't need your mum in my ear to know you haven't quite been yourself the last few days.
AARON: You mean since Donny died.
BUSHY: Unless there's some other shitful thing been going on that I don't know about, then yes. That's exactly what I mean.

　　AARON *doesn't reply. He sits.*

It's okay. I haven't been myself either. Grief's a funny thing. It'll sneak up on you. You do your best to put a kid on the right track… [*Realising*] Sorry, bad choice of words. Sometimes a kid slips through the net. Still, you try, but you can't always tell, you know?
AARON: Tell what? You mean me?
BUSHY: You, Donny, me. Everyone. We're all mysteries, would you say?

　　AARON *doesn't want to talk.*

Actually you're half right. I have been talkin' to your mum. But not about you. I like her, your mum. Your dad's okay too, but your mum's special.

　　AARON *shoots him a look.*

I don't mean like that. I mean she's a smart woman. She's pretty cut up about this Donny business.
AARON: Bit late for that.
BUSHY: She's not responsible, Aaron. She never meant for anything bad to happen to him. He did that all on his own.

　　They sit for a moment. AARON *looks at the box.*

You and Desley still playing in that band?

　　AARON *nods.*

Thought I heard somewhere you were having a crack at Unearthed?
AARON: Maybe.
BUSHY: Good on you. Good luck.
AARON: It's not for certain yet.
BUSHY: You got a demo?

AARON *nods.*

I'll get my Year Nine's to play it on the school radio.
AARON: Your Year Nines aren't gonna want to hear our music.
BUSHY: People never know what they want to hear until they hear it. 'Specially Year Nines.

Long beat.

AARON: Can I go?

BUSHY *moves out of his way, but as* AARON *gets to the door…*
BUSHY: You don't want to know what's in the box?

AARON *stops.*

You know I used to play AFL?

AARON *shrugs.*

Played three games for Fitzroy.
AARON: Bullshit. They're not even a team.
BUSHY: Yeah, well. That's another story.
AARON: You ever play in a Grand Final?
BUSHY: Nah. I kicked a goal at the MCG though. Big game. Into time-on. Took a screamer and won the match. Thought I was king dick. Was gonna be the next Jezza.
AARON: Who?
BUSHY: Never mind.
AARON: What happened?
BUSHY: Did my knee. Spent the rest of the season out injured. Never got picked again. Took up ballroom dancing as part of my rehabilitation. Got pretty good at it too. Anyway, after he knew I wasn't gonna play football anymore, the coach came up to me and he gave me that box.
AARON: What's in it?
BUSHY: That's what I said.
AARON: And?
BUSHY: He told me to open it.

AARON *opens the box and takes out a cigar.*

You know what that is?
AARON: A cigar.
BUSHY: A Cuban cigar. You know where Cuba is?

AARON *shakes his head.*

Go on. Take a good strong whiff. There's nothing like the smell of a Cuban cigar.

AARON *sniffs the cigar.*

You know what they say about Cuban cigars?

AARON *shakes his head.* BUSHY *moves in close to* AARON... *secretively.*

They say the leaves are rolled on the thighs of virgins.

AARON *hands it back to* BUSHY, *a bit embarrassed.*

Personally, I think it's bullshit. Nice fantasy, though. So, where was I?

AARON *sits back down, curious now.*

AARON: You did your knee.

BUSHY: So I did. And I'm standin' there with my leg bandaged all the way up to my arsehole, and the coach holds up this cigar and says to me, 'Bushy. You probably feel like shit right now. But pretty soon you'll find something else that'll make you feel good again, and when you do, I want you to smoke this stogie and remember just how shit you felt when I gave it to you. I guarantee, you're not gonna feel this bad forever.'

AARON: So how come you never smoked it? You just always feel like shit?

BUSHY: Nah. The coach was right. Good things happened. But every time they did, I felt like something better might still be to come. And that always makes me feel... [*taking a big sniff of the cigar*] optimistic. And even when things weren't so hot, I still had it there, kind of like a promise that things would eventually get better. It's become a bit of a talisman for me. You know what a talisman is?

AARON *nods.*

I guess you're pretty upset about Donny. You and him were mates, weren't you?

AARON: [*getting up*] I gotta go.

BUSHY *sizes* AARON *up for a bit. He decides to let it go for now.*

BUSHY: Don't let me stop you. Tell you what, though. You hang onto that cigar for a bit.

AARON: How come?
BUSHY: Who knows. Maybe you'll find the right occasion. Maybe we'll smoke it together some night, in honour of optimism.
AARON: But it's yours, Bushy. You should be the one to smoke it.
BUSHY: At the rate I'm going it'll disintegrate before I decide to smoke it. You try it out for a while. Let me know what you think. I've got to go and beat some education into those Year Nine shitbags.

>AARON *is a bit bemused.* BUSHY *leaves.*

>And if you tell your mum I said that, I'll tell her what you did on the Year Eight camp.

AARON: [*calling after him*] I didn't do anything on the Year Eight camp.
BUSHY: [*calling back*] Who's she gonna believe?

>AARON *leaves, taking the cigar with him.*

SCENE SIX

Thursday afternoon.

RITA *is in the staff room writing her speech for the funeral.*

MR DONNEL *hurries in, looking for something.*

MR DONNEL: You seen my mug?
RITA: [*not really interested*] Not on its hook?
MR DONNEL: I wouldn't be asking if it was on its hook.
RITA: Try the freezer.
MR DONNEL: The freezer?
RITA: [*impatient with him*] The cleaners put 'em in the freezer if you don't put 'em back on their hooks.
MR DONNEL: Fascists. [*He finds his mug.*] Oh, it's cracked. Bastards.

>*He pinches someone else's mug and comes over to the table. He rifles through* RITA*'s pencil case, finds a marker, crosses out the name on the mug and writes his own.*

>I tell you. We don't often see eye to eye. I know that. But giving that kid the boot? As far as I'm concerned, it was the smartest thing you've ever done.

RITA: What?
MR DONNEL: The jumper.
RITA: Don't call him that. Nobody's saying that's what happened.

MR DONNEL: Yeah, well tomayto, tomarto. Point being, giving him the arse sent a message to the rest of the students, if they want to act like shits they get treated like shit. You showed good leadership, Rita. You made an example of him. And then he went and made an example of himself.

RITA: He was just a boy who broke a rule.

MR DONNEL: Bullshit. Your Aaron's just a boy. Donny was a lazy, smart-arse, no-hoper. A waste of space. A tragic life just waiting to happen, and in the end, he didn't have to wait all that long, did he?

RITA: I'm sure some people made it seem like quite a long time.

MR DONNEL: Yeah, well I'll tell you another thing for nothing. I'm not giving my geography class the morning off to go to that little turd's funeral. You go and weep crocodile tears over him if you like, but he's not going to waste the time of my good students anymore. He did enough of that when he was here.

RITA: They were his friends, Clive. They have a right to be there.

MR DONNEL: They have a right to an education, that's what they have a right to.

RITA: And you don't think this is something they should learn about?

MR DONNEL: No, I don't. The problem with this school is that we spend too much time spoon-feeding the failures, instead of giving them the kick up the arse they deserve. We don't single out the best students and make a big deal out of their achievements, because we might upset the no-hopers like Donny. It brings us all down to the lowest common denominator.

RITA: That's enough.

MR DONNEL: No it's not.

RITA: [*in his face*] Yes it is.

MR DONNEL: [*up for a fight*] No it's not. We're always listening to you shooting your mouth off. Well you can bloody well listen to what I've got to say for once.

> *He thrusts a pile of report cards at her.* BUSHY *comes in, hangs back, enjoying himself.*

Look at these. We're not allowed to give an A student an A and an F student an F. We've gotta put it in some stupid bloody code. You make us write all this encouraging bullshit so it doesn't affect their self-esteem. Well, some of these kids don't deserve self-esteem.

They haven't earned it. This crap didn't work on Donny, and it won't work on any of these other no-hopers. So you do what you like, but my kids'll be sitting an exam tomorrow, and if they're failures they'll know about it 'cos there'll be a big red F on their paper.

> DESLEY *enters.* RITA *doesn't see her. She's too furious with* MR DONNEL.

RITA: Don't you talk about our students like that. I will decide who goes to Donny's funeral. So keep your ignorant, small-minded opinions to yourself. No-one here cares what you think.

> MR DONNEL *is lost for words. He sees* BUSHY. *He turns and sees* DESLEY. *They are both embarrassed.*

DESLEY: Hello, Mr Donnell

> *He storms out.* RITA *composes herself.* DESLEY *tries to keep from smiling.* RITA *too.* BUSHY *keeps out of the way.*

RITA: I'm sorry, Desley. You shouldn't have had to witness that.
DESLEY: I can come back tomorrow.
RITA: No, that's okay. Come in.
DESLEY: I wanted to… Can I ask you something?
RITA: Of course. Anything.
DESLEY: I just wanted to ask if you'd write me a reference.
RITA: Are you going for a job? You're not leaving school?
DESLEY: No. Not until the end of the year. I'm thinking of going for a cadetship with the *Courier*. I thought if I had a good reference and sent them some of my writing, they might take me on next year.

> RITA *gives* DESLEY *a big hug.*

RITA: Desley, that's fantastic. I'm so proud of you. Of course I'll write you a reference. Do you want me to give the editor a call? I could…
DESLEY: The reference'll be fine. There's no real hurry. After the deb ball will do.

> *She leaves.* BUSHY *is about to say something, when* DESLEY *comes back in.*

Sorry, I didn't… I meant to say… thanks.
RITA: Of course.

> *This time she really leaves.*

BUSHY: She looks up to you.
RITA: It's just a reference. [*Beat.*] You don't think I should be encouraging her to look further afield?
BUSHY: She'll be fine. She's got more going for her than most of these other kids put together.
RITA: Isn't that a reason to get out of a small town?
BUSHY: We're both still here. We did alright for ourselves.
RITA: If you say so.
BUSHY: It's only smart kids like Desley who can make a real go of it in a place as small as this. It's the average ones who need the big cities. They need the options.

> RITA *and* BUSHY *leave. They seem to be on speaking terms again.*

SCENE SEVEN

Thursday night.

RITA *is sitting on her bed, still trying to write her speech.*

A sound from outside.

RITA: Is that Aaron home?
REG: [*offstage*] No. Just putting the rubbish out.
RITA: Perhaps one of us should wait up for him.

> REG *comes in, dressing-gown and boots. He sits on the other end of the bed.*

REG: He'll be alright. I've left the front light on.
RITA: Have you talked to him yet?
REG: Not yet.
RITA: I really think you should talk to him, Reg.
REG: I will.
RITA: It's important for a boy to be able to speak with his father.
REG: It's important for him to be able to speak to both of us.
RITA: I can't do everything on my own, Reg.
REG: I said I'd talk to him.
RITA: Yes, well. Soon.
REG: Are you alright?
RITA: I'm fine. Tired. I'm fine.
REG: [*looking at what she's writing*] Is this what you're going to say?

RITA: You'd think I'd be able to come up with a simple speech.
REG: Maybe it's not so simple. I wouldn't know where to begin.

They sit together, but apart, for a moment.

You remember that spot by the creek in the bottom paddock? Where we used to go for picnics?
RITA: When the kids were little.
REG: When we were still driving my old man's Zephyr.

They laugh at the memory.

I was thinking. If Sharon comes home for Christmas, maybe we should go back there for a picnic lunch. A real bush Christmas.
RITA: It's not our place anymore.
REG: I know. But I could give 'em a call. They wouldn't mind. It'd just be the four of us.
RITA: It's a nice idea, Reg.
REG: You used to like my ideas.

An uncertain moment between them.

So I'll give 'em a call. See what they say. [*He looks at the speech.*] Maybe you should get someone else to do it. If it's going to upset you.
RITA: Why doesn't anyone think I'm capable of doing this?
REG: It's not that. It's just… if it's going to make you…
RITA: We can't all just throw our hands up in the air and fall in a heap because life gets too hard. Someone has to be the grown-up.

REG *is hurt, like he's been slapped in the face. He turns to leave.*

Where are you going?
REG: You're right. [*Beat.*] Someone should wait up for Aaron.

REG *goes out.*

SCENE EIGHT

Friday morning.

AARON *comes into the kitchen, dumps his bag on the table. He rifles through, finds a notebook and a bag of dope. He takes them into his room.*

He turns on his music. One of his band's songs plays. He lights up, kicks back and scribbles in his notebook.

REG comes in wearing his crossing supervisor uniform. He takes his gear off and hangs it up. He stops, listens to AARON's song.

REG comes back to the table, sees AARON's bag. Without thinking, he goes through it, pulling out objects—a digital videotape, the cigar box, a book—it's not like he's looking to find anything in particular. It's like he's getting to know his son.

He notices a scrap of paper poking out of the book. He reads what's written on it, looks towards AARON's room, re-reads it and absently slips it into his shirt pocket.

He sits, stares off into space. AARON sits, stares off into space.

AARON gets up, puts on his tie and jacket for the funeral, turns the music off, comes into the kitchen. He's a bit stoned.

REG: You going now?
AARON: Yeah.

    REG nods to himself. AARON goes to leave again.

REG: Was that one of yours you were playing?
AARON: Yeah.
REG: It was good. Did you write it?
AARON: Yeah.
REG: You're doing that radio thing? Diggin' It?

    AARON tries to stifle a laugh.

Did I say something funny?
AARON: [*laughing*] It's called Unearthed, Dad.
REG: [*doesn't see the joke*] Yeah. You're doing that, then?

    AARON makes a serious face. He shrugs and nods.

Good on you. [*Beat.*] Did I tell you I'm giving Allan a hand, blowing out a new dam? Gotta pick up the gelignite, set the charges, that sort of thing. You could come along, if you're not doing anything. I'll show you how it's done. Take a couple a beers or something. Just the two boys together. We could do a bit of rabbitting afterwards. Break out the old rifle.

    The two men look at each other. They just can't find their connection.

AARON: Sure, Dad. Whatever. I gotta go.

REG *watches his boy go.*

REG: Righteo then.

REG's attention drifts. There's something on the table leg that isn't right... a loose screw or something. He picks at it with his finger, bends down to take a closer look.

When he sits up he's in the doctor's office.

SCENE NINE

Friday, late morning.

REG *sits, fidgeting. He breathes heavily. He waits.*

GILLIAN, *the doctor, comes in.*

GILLIAN: Sorry to keep you waiting... [*checking her file*]... Reg.
REG: [*rising halfway out of his seat*] Doctor...?
GILLIAN: Gillian.
REG: Gillian. [*He sits.*] I'm surprised you're in today. Considering.
GILLIAN: One doctor for the whole district. It's not that easy to take a day off.
REG: Never been to a lady doctor before.

REG, *awkward, starts to unbutton his shirt.*

GILLIAN: We button on the other side.

REG *stops, looks at his buttons.*

REG: Oh.
GILLIAN: I'm sorry. A joke. You can leave your shirt on for the moment, if you like.
REG: Oh. Righteo, then.

He does his buttons up again.

GILLIAN: So what I can do for you today?

He reaches into his shirt pocket and pulls out an empty tablet box. It has AARON*'s scrap of paper folded in with it.*

REG: I've run out of these.

As he hands over the box, he separates the scrap of paper from it.

GILLIAN: Dr Atkinson wrote this for you?

REG: The old doc, yeah. Blood pressure was up a bit.
GILLIAN: And you ran out when?
REG: Not long. A week. Maybe two.
GILLIAN: We might do a routine exam.
REG: Righteo, then.

> GILLIAN *feels his pulse, takes his temperature, looks in his ears… that sort of thing.*

GILLIAN: You live in town?
REG: [*nodding*] Do now. Used to run dairy cattle. A small place up above the floodplain. Had to give it away. Drought got us in the end. My boy, Aaron, would've been the fifth generation to make a living out of that place. If I'd been able to make a go of it. [*He shrugs.*] Some things aren't meant to be, eh.
GILLIAN: How do you find it? Living in town?
REG: Yeah, it's okay. Used to be hard on my wife, when she went back to teaching. Help out with finances, you know. Hour or more's drive each way. Much easier on her now.
GILLIAN: And you?
REG: Change is as good as a holiday, isn't that what they say?
GILLIAN: Is it?
REG: Yeah. I mean it's not the same. Work's not easy to find when you're my age. Don't know much more than farming. I get by, I s'pose.
GILLIAN: You do the crossing at the primary school.
REG: Lollipop Man. That's right.
GILLIAN: Roll up your sleeve.

> *She gets out the blood pressure pump.*

REG: Saw a show on the telly about blood pressure. Well, not about blood pressure exactly. It was about a machine this bloke invented. A kind of lie detector. It could tell you when a person's not saying what they mean by measuring their blood pressure. You have to admire a bloke who can build something like that from scratch.
GILLIAN: I don't get time for television.
REG: You're not missing much.

> *She looks at the blood pressure gauge, then at* REG, *who avoids her glance.*

GILLIAN: It's quite high. How're you sleeping?

REG: [*with a shrug*] On and off, you know. Town's a bit noisier. I miss the quiet. Used to find it hard waking up for the four a.m. milking. Now I'm wide awake at four every night. You think there's something wrong with that?

GILLIAN: As you say, town's noisier. How's your diet?

REG: [*worried*] I'm not on a diet.

GILLIAN: Eating habits. Do you eat okay?

REG: I'm not a big eater, if that's what you mean.

GILLIAN: Do you drink? Smoke?

REG: Gave the smokes away years ago. Don't mind a beer.

GILLIAN: Every day?

REG: [*winking*] A quiet one or two helps me wind down.

GILLIAN: We might look at changing your medication.

REG: You're the doctor.

> *He watches her making notes in his file. He fidgets with the scrap of paper.*

Guess it's all in there, eh. Everything that's wrong with me.

GILLIAN: I wouldn't put it quite like that.

> REG *watches her, wanting to say something.*

REG: That boy that died. The business at the bridge.

> *She keeps writing.*

You're related, aren't you?

> *She writes his prescription.* REG *folds and unfolds the paper.*

GILLIAN: My sister's boy.

REG: Young kid like that. A real tragedy. He was a friend of my son's, you know. How's she taking it? Your sister?

GILLIAN: She's... angry.

REG: I don't know what Rita and me'd do if Aaron ever did... if something like that happened to Aaron.

> *She hands* REG *his prescription.*

GILLIAN: Let's hope you never have to find out.

> *She packs her things away.* REG *makes no move to leave.*

Was there something else?

REG fidgets with the scrap of paper, then holds it out to her.

REG: What d'you make of this?

She reads the paper.

My boy wrote it. Song lyrics.

GILLIAN: I can see.

She hands the paper back to REG.

Strong images.

REG shrugs, embarrassed and helpless.

You're concerned for him?

REG: [*nodding*] You got kids?

She shakes her head.

You do your best for them. I just don't know what he wants.

GILLIAN: Have you talked with him?

REG: You sound like my wife.

GILLIAN: Have you?

REG: [*with a shrug*] They're hard work, the young blokes?

GILLIAN: It's important to keep the lines of communication open.

REG: He should come in here, have a chat with you.

GILLIAN: I'd be happy to see him. But I think you should talk with him first. It'd be much better for the both of you.

REG: [*with half a smile*] You're the doctor.

GILLIAN: So you said.

REG goes to leave.

Don't forget your prescription.

REG scoops it up from the table.

REG: Forget my head if it wasn't screwed on.

He goes to thank her, awkward with a woman. She sticks her hand out. REG *shakes it.*

Good on ya, doc.

REG hesitates for a moment, then leaves. GILLIAN *watches him go.*

SCENE TEN

Friday afternoon.

AARON *bursts out of* DONNY*'s funeral, distressed. He can't listen to any more.*

AARON: [*to himself*] Fuck. Fuck. [*He turns and shouts.*] Fuckin' hypocrites!

> *He walks in circles then stops, half sits, half collapses on the ground. He sits there, shaking his head and wiping his eyes.*
>
> *After a few moments,* DESLEY *follows him out.*

I'm okay.

DESLEY: No you're not.

AARON: It's just... it was starting to freak me out. How can she say that? How can she lie like that?

DESLEY: It's what people say.

AARON: It's bullshit. [*He tries to laugh.*] I bet it's the first time Donny's ever been in a church.

> *They sit in silence.*

I've never been to a funeral before. They always like that?

DESLEY: I s'pose so. 'Cept at my foster mum's funeral I kind of believed what people said.

> AARON *is struggling to stay in control. He pulls out his bag of dope. It's more than half empty.* DESLEY *looks concerned for him.*

Not here, Aaron.

> *He puts it away.*

AARON: Good old Des. Wouldn't want to be inappropriate.

DESLEY: Maybe you should go and see someone.

AARON: I don't want to see anyone.

DESLEY: I mean get some help.

AARON: What, a shrink? I'm fine, Des. I got upset. My friend's dead and my mum's standing up there... I'm just upset, that's all.

DESLEY: Doesn't have to be a shrink. Go see the doctor.

AARON: Might as well take an ad out in the *Courier*. For those who didn't already know, Aaron's fucked in the head.

DESLEY: You might get some better drugs.
AARON: I don't think they give out those sort of drugs.
DESLEY: Wouldn't hurt. It might help.
AARON: How come you're the expert?

>   *She shrugs.*

Did you go?
DESLEY: For a while.
AARON: And?
DESLEY: It was okay. It was good.
AARON: They make you talk?
DESLEY: They don't make you do anything.
AARON: They'd make me talk.
DESLEY: It's not like you're dobbing someone in, Aaron. It's only about you. About how you feel.
AARON: Why's everyone so interested in how I feel?
DESLEY: Sometimes it's good, just to say stuff, even to a stranger. Especially to a stranger.
AARON: Yeah, well what if you don't know how you feel? What if you don't feel anything?
DESLEY: Then that's what you tell 'em.
AARON: They don't give up that easy.
DESLEY: People just want to help.
AARON: I don't want their help.
DESLEY: I want to help.
AARON: I just want to be left alone.

>   DESLEY *gives up and moves away from him.*

I don't mean you, Des.
DESLEY: I should go back in.
AARON: This is so fucked.

>   AARON *runs off. After a moment,* RITA *comes out of the church.*

RITA: Where is he?
DESLEY: Gone.
RITA: How could he walk out on his friend like that?
DESLEY: He wasn't walking out on Donny.

>   RITA *looks around.*

RITA: Where is he, Des?
DESLEY: He'll be up at the bridge.
RITA: You going after him?
DESLEY: [*shaking her head*] You should go.

> RITA *looks back towards the church, torn.*

They don't need you in there.
RITA: You know, Donny never even came to our house.
DESLEY: He wasn't that kind of friend.

> RITA *can't make up her mind She looks back towards the church again.*

RITA: Aaron's dad…
DESLEY: I'll tell him.

> DESLEY *goes back into the church. After a moment,* RITA *goes after* AARON.

SCENE ELEVEN

Friday afternoon.

AARON *comes onto the bridge. He lights a joint and starts writing in his notebook.*

RITA *comes onto the bridge.* AARON *looks up and sees his mother. Neither speak. Then…*

AARON: Go away.

> RITA *stays.*

I said go away. I don't want you.

> *She moves closer.*

What are you doing here?
RITA: You left before they took Donny away.
AARON: You mean I missed the end of your bullshit speech.
RITA: I mean I was worried about you.
AARON: Yeah, well don't be.
RITA: I just want to…
AARON: What? You just want to what? Spout more shit about how much you all cared about Donny.

> *He flicks his joint at her.*

He was my friend, not yours. Pretending you gave a shit about him, sending flowers to his mum, saying all that stuff at his funeral. If you cared so much about him, why'd you give him the arse?

RITA: He stole school property.

AARON: That's not what happened.

RITA: He stole a camera. An expensive camera.

AARON: He borrowed it. You just had it in for him. You don't deserve to be at his funeral. None of you do. [*He holds up his notebook.*] If you were his friend, then you'd know these things. [*He jumps up and delivers a mock eulogy.*] Ten things no-one said at Donny's funeral. One. Donny was an arsehole. Two. He could be okay sometimes. Three. He had sex when he was thirteen. Four. He always knew where to get dope. Five. He showed me how to do the drawback. Six. He did a shit-hot impression of Mr Donnel: 'You're all no-hopers, you pack of little turds. Especially you, Donny.' Everyone in town thought Donny was a write-off. He couldn't write for shit but he had lots of good ideas. He did a lot of bad shit but he wasn't a thief. He was gonna make a movie and I was gonna do the music. That's why he borrowed the camera. Borrowed it. And he would've brought it back.

RITA: It wasn't just the camera, Aaron. He was out of control. He started fights with the younger students, he was abusive to teachers, he made threats when he didn't get his own way. I gave him every chance, Aaron. He made his choice… and in the end I had to make mine. I had the whole school to think of. Donny was just thinking of himself.

AARON: You don't know what Donny was thinking. You're so full of shit.

  AARON *and* RITA *haven't noticed that* REG *has arrived.*

REG: That's enough, Aaron.

AARON: Oh, look out. Nobody run. The Lollipop Man's here.

REG: I said that's enough.

AARON: What're gonna do? Hold up your 'Stop' sign?

REG: I think we should go home.

AARON: I'm not going anywhere.

REG: I think you need to spend some time at home.

AARON: What about her? When's she gonna spend time at home?

REG: Don't speak about your mother like that.
AARON: Fine. I'll keep my fuckin' mouth shut like everyone else in this family.
REG: Just calm down, mate.
AARON: You don't get to call me mate.
RITA: Reg, let's just go.
AARON: Good idea. Why don't you both just fuck off.
REG: I've had just about enough of you.
AARON: What are you gonna do about it, Lollipop Man?

> RITA *tries to calm* REG, *to pull him away, but he shakes her off.*

You're such a loser.
REG: Take that back.
RITA: Reg!
REG: I said take it back.
AARON: Loser.

> *That's it for* REG. *He loses control and throws a punch.*
>
> AARON *falls to the ground.*
>
> *Blackout.*

END OF ACT ONE

ACT TWO

SCENE TWELVE

Wednesday afternoon.

AARON *stands with his back to the room, looking out of the window.*

GILLIAN *enters, watches him for a moment, moves to the table.*

GILLIAN: Would you like to sit, Aaron?
AARON: No.
GILLIAN: You said on the phone you'd been having trouble sleeping.
AARON: Yeah.
GILLIAN: Anything else besides not being able to sleep?
AARON: I feel like shit.
GILLIAN: Is that all?

> AARON *turns. He's sporting a pretty good black eye.* GILLIAN *can't help but notice.*

AARON: I've been getting headaches.
GILLIAN: I'm not surprised.
AARON: It's not from this.
GILLIAN: Is it a sharp, stabbing kind of pain, or a dull thud?
AARON: The second one.
GILLIAN: Bad?

> AARON *nods.* GILLIAN *writes something on a pad.*

AARON: What're you writing?
GILLIAN: I'm just taking notes.
AARON: Can I see?

> *She pushes the pad across the table.* AARON *comes over, sits, reads, seems satisfied, pushes it back to her. She continues her note-taking.*

GILLIAN: How long have you felt like this? Like shit.
AARON: I dunno. A while. It's been worse lately. Since…
GILLIAN: When was the last time you felt good?

AARON *thinks for a bit, remembering.*

AARON: Maybe last summer.

GILLIAN: What happened last summer?

AARON: I stayed with my sister. In the city. Took the train. She promised my mum and dad she'd keep an eye on me. [*He laughs.*] Be my chaperone. Like that was gonna happen. She's got a spare room. Let me have my own key. I got out. Saw some bands. It was like… it was good. I felt good.

Beat.

GILLIAN: What do you think causes them? The headaches.

AARON: I thought you'd be able to tell me. [*He goes back to the window.*] I can't stop thinking.

GILLIAN: What about?

AARON: I dunno. About everything.

GILLIAN *waits.*

About Donny. You saw him, didn't you?

GILLIAN: In circumstances like these, the law requires me to conduct a full medical examination of the deceased.

AARON: You mean Donny.

GILLIAN: Yes, Donny.

AARON: What'd he look like?

GILLIAN *doesn't answer.*

I can't stop thinking about… what'd he look like?

GILLIAN *opens a drawer and takes out a copy of* DONNY's *autopsy report, reads from it.*

GILLIAN: It would appear that Donny left the bridge and struck the carriage roof. In doing so, he sustained a severe trauma to the back of his skull. He then fell to the ground, sustaining major internal injuries resulting in massive organ failure… although it was probably the fractured skull which killed him.

AARON *looks at the report in her hand. Looks at* GILLIAN. *Against her better judgement, she hands it to him.* AARON *reads over the report. After a bit…*

AARON: This says 'Death by misadventure'. Does that mean it wasn't an accident?

GILLIAN: It means he didn't take enough responsibility for himself to prevent his own death.

>AARON *thinks about this for a moment.*

AARON: You're his aunty, aren't you?

>GILLIAN *nods.*

Shit.

>AARON *gives the report back, sits.*

I don't understand why it happened.

GILLIAN: It would have been over very quickly.

AARON: You must see lots of dead people.

GILLIAN: Some.

AARON: You wouldn't usually know them, though.

GILLIAN: Not usually.

AARON: I used to be a bit scared of Donny. Lots of kids were. You ever had a friend that you sort of liked and didn't like at the same time?

>GILLIAN *nods.*

He wasn't really like… not the way people thought of him.

GILLIAN: Donny sometimes found it hard to fit in.

AARON: I miss him.

GILLIAN: It's good that he had a friend like you, Aaron. [*Beat.*] I'm going to write you a prescription for your headaches. It'll probably help you sleep a bit better, too. You shouldn't mix these with alcohol, or take them with any other drugs. Do you know what I mean?

>AARON *looks away, but nods.*

AARON: Can you write me a note, too?

>GILLIAN *doesn't understand what he means.*

In case someone asks me what I was doing here. Just say I've got the flu or a twenty-four hour virus or something like that. You know? Something normal.

GILLIAN: This is very normal, Aaron.

AARON: Write it anyway? Please?

GILLIAN: I'd like to see you again. Follow up on those headaches. Early next week.

AARON: Sure.

GILLIAN *sizes up* AARON, *smiles, writes a note.*

GILLIAN: How does non-specific cerebral duress sound?

AARON *doesn't know what the fuck she's talking about, but it sounds pretty good.*

AARON: Cool.

He leaves.

SCENE THIRTEEN

Thursday afternoon.

DESLEY *is waiting, getting impatient.*

AARON *enters. He's antsy, agitated. He roams the room, avoiding eye contact with her.*

DESLEY: I didn't think you were coming.
AARON: I said I'd be here.
DESLEY: You should have been here twenty minutes ago.
AARON: I'm here now, aren't I?
DESLEY: Are you?

AARON *gives her a smart-arse look.*

AARON: Where's Bushy? I can't be that late if Bushy's not here.
DESLEY: He went to give you a call. Apparently you're getting a reputation for being a bit of a no-show.
AARON: What's that s'posed to mean?
DESLEY: Skipping school.
AARON: I've been sick.
DESLEY: You didn't turn up for work. You missed band practice.
AARON: Haven't you got anything better to do than run around checking up on me? You're not my mum, Des. You wouldn't want to be.
DESLEY: Don't knock your mum, Aaron. At least she makes the effort.
AARON: Yeah, well you can have her.
DESLEY: Yeah, well maybe if you didn't have a mum, you wouldn't be such a dick about it.

AARON *realises that he has put his foot in it, but he can't bring himself to say sorry.*

I'm worried about you.

AARON: You and everyone else. I'm fine. I did what you wanted. I went to see the doctor. Why can't everyone leave me alone?

They are both silent for a moment.

DESLEY: If you don't want to do this, just say so.

Nothing.

At least be honest with me.

AARON: I don't feel much like dancing.

DESLEY: What's that supposed to mean?

AARON: It means you might be better off finding someone else.

DESLEY: You're a bastard, Aaron.

She goes to leave. AARON *stops her.*

AARON: You told me to be honest.

DESLEY: You promised me you'd do it.

AARON: You said it, Des. I'm a bastard. What d'you want to do your deb with me for anyway? Find some guy you're really interested in.

DESLEY: I'm interested in you.

AARON: I mean seriously interested.

DESLEY: You don't think I'm interested?

AARON: You know you're not. I know you're not.

DESLEY: And what? You are?

AARON: I didn't say that.

DESLEY: [*mocking him*] You want me to be *seriously* interested in you, Aaron?

AARON: Don't fuck around, Des. I'm not in the mood.

DESLEY: So what *are* you in the mood for?

   DESLEY *starts to make playful, teasing moves on* AARON.

AARON: Don't, Des. I mean it.

He tries hard not to enter into the spirit of it, but she wins him over.

DESLEY: Pleeease do my deb with me, Aaron.

The sound of a diesel train in the distance slowly becomes music. It becomes a 'train-waltz' heard far away.

DESLEY *starts to dance around* AARON. *He tries to maintain his sullen mood, but his old self can't help seeping through.*

As the music gets closer, AARON *begins to smile.*

Pleeease. You won't regret it.
AARON: I already do.
DESLEY: Dance with me, Aaron.

> *She takes his hand. He resists for a moment, but the music swells and he gets swept away in it. As* AARON *gets taken by the music, they both dance in a joyous moment that releases them from everything that has happened since* DONNY *died.*

Still don't feel like dancing?
AARON: I don't know what I feel.
DESLEY: Are we still friends?
AARON: Of course we are, Des.
DESLEY: Even if I'm not *seriously* interested?
AARON: Especially if you're not seriously interested.
DESLEY: So you'll do the deb?
AARON: You're trying to manipulate me.
DESLEY: I know. Is it working?
AARON: I don't know.
DESLEY: You promised me.
AARON: I know.
DESLEY: So you'll keep your promise?

> BUSHY *enters in a Shakespearean demeanour.*

BUSHY: And his promises were, as he then was, mighty.

> *A waltz begins.*
>
> BUSHY *holds out an arm to them, beckoning them to join him. They can't ignore him. They can't resist him.*
>
> DESLEY *cracks up first, then* AARON, *and eventually the two of them are really laughing. They are drawn into* BUSHY's *dance until all three of them are swirling to the music and laughing their heads off.*
>
> *The three of them dance a Pride of Erin together.*
>
> *Then* BUSHY *dances with* DESLEY *while* AARON *tries to copy their movements.*
>
> BUSHY *dances her out of the space, leaving* AARON *going through the steps on his own.*
>
> *The sound of a diesel train in the distance.*

SCENE FOURTEEN

Friday morning.

AARON *is at home again.*

RITA *enters carrying a suit bag.* AARON *ignores her. She goes into his room.*

REG *enters.* AARON *ignores him too.*

REG *goes to his crossing supervisor uniform and starts to put it on.*

In Aaron's room, RITA *finds his pills. She comes back out, still with the suit bag.*

RITA: What are these?

AARON: The doctor gave them to me.

RITA: And were you going to tell me?

AARON: I don't have to tell you.

> REG *is on his way out, 'Stop' sign in hand.*

RITA: [*to* REG] Are you going to say something, or do I have to do this on my own?

REG: He's old enough to make his own choices.

RITA: That's your idea of being a father, is it? Leave him to work everything out for himself.

REG: I just don't think we can make all his decisions for him.

RITA: Are you that hollow? Is that all you have to offer?

REG: I have to go to work.

> REG *leaves.* RITA *watches him go, calms down, moves to her son.*

RITA: I'm sorry. I was just disappointed that you didn't consult me first.

AARON: Yeah, well I'm disappointed about a lot of things too. Life sucks, in case you hadn't noticed. What are you going to do about it? Expel me? Expel the doctor?

RITA: Maybe it's time you faced up to a few things.

AARON: Like what?

RITA: Sometimes we have to do things that we don't want to. People who break the rules get punished.

AARON: You mean Donny, or me?

RITA: I didn't do it out of spite, Aaron.

AARON: He didn't steal it. He borrowed it.

RITA: He didn't have permission to borrow it. That makes it stealing.
AARON: If he'd asked you, would you have lent it to him?

    RITA *doesn't have an answer.*

What if it had been me?
RITA: Things aren't always so straightforward, Aaron.
AARON: Not for people like Donny they're not.
RITA: I feel like shit about Donny. I'm not saying what happened was my fault. It wasn't. But I do wish I'd taken more time with him. He deserved that, at least. You deserve it. I know I haven't talked with you about Donny. I know I haven't made the time. But I will. I want to.

    AARON *says nothing.* RITA *picks up the pill bottle.*

At least tell me what they're for?

    AARON *pulls out his note from the doctor, hands it to* RITA.

AARON: They're to help me with my distress.
RITA: Your what?
AARON: I've got something called… [*Can't quite remember*] 'cervical distress'.

    RITA *is still angry, but she can't help but find his mistake funny.*

RITA: I'm glad you're doing the deb.
AARON: I'm only doing it for Des.

    RITA *holds the suit up against him.*

RITA: Still. I'm glad. You and Des are going to look lovely together.
AARON: There's nothing going on, Mum. Me and Desley are just…
RITA: I know. But still…

    She hugs him. AARON *squirms.*

It's going to make me very proud.

    AARON *takes the suit bag and goes into his room.*

    RITA *leaves.*

SCENE FIFTEEN

Friday afternoon.

AARON *is getting ready for the deb, putting on his dress shirt and tie.*

Halfway through, he stops. He turns, picks up the video camera. He turns it over in his hands, like he's trying to nut it out, then pops it open and takes out the cartridge. He sits, staring at the cartridge.

Lights up on…

REG *is at the school crossing dressed in his lollipop uniform.*

He stands in the middle of the road, holding his 'Stop' sign. The kids have all gone home. He's lost, in a kind of trance.

Lights up on…

DESLEY *comes into her room with her deb dress.*

She touches the fabric. She holds it up to her body and dances with it as though it's her partner. She beams in her fantasy. She slips the dress on over her clothes, stands in front of the mirror and looks at herself in the dress. Slowly the fantasy slips away. The dress is constricting and uncomfortable. She starts to tug the material away from her body. It gets worse.

DESLEY *rips the dress off and runs out.*

At the crossing, REG *is oblivious to sound of an approaching car. It roars down the street towards him.*

HOONS [*voice-over*]: Get out of the road, you fuckin' idiot.

> *The hoon-mobile speeds past* REG. *He stares down the road, lets his 'Stop' sign droop, lets out a heavy, helpless sigh, and walks off.*

In his room, AARON *comes to a decision. He starts to pack his bag.*

SCENE SIXTEEN

Friday evening.

REG *sits at the kitchen table in his crossing supervisor's uniform.*

AARON *grabs his bag and guitar and comes out of his room dressed in jeans, sneakers, his dress shirt and jacket. He is surprised to find his father there.*

AARON: What are you doing, Dad?

> REG *doesn't answer, distracted. He is cleaning an old rifle.*

REG: Your grandpa used to take me rabbitting when I was your age.

We'd set out just before first light. It's the best time, you know. Just as the sun comes up, dew all over the grass, while they're still out of their burrows. Some blokes reckon you're better to go later, after they've bedded down. Use ferrets to flush 'em out, but my dad never liked ferrets. Called 'em burrow-rats. Nasty, runts of things they are. [*His attention goes back to cleaning the gun. After a bit he continues his story.*] I used to love those early mornings. Your grandpa would tell me stories about growing up on the farm, how his father taught him to use a gun. It was like there was no-one else in the world but him and me. He never spoke much around the house, but when we'd go out rabbitting, it was like he was a different man. You couldn't shut him up. It was like our secret time together.

AARON: Dad? What are you doing?

> REG's *attention is suddenly back in the room.*

REG: Getting ready. You're still coming, aren't you?
AARON: What d'you mean?
REG: Like we said. Just the two boys, together.
AARON: You're not making any sense.
REG: Rabbitting. Tomorrow. After we blow out the dam at Allan's.
AARON: I never said I was coming.
REG: Oh…
AARON: I have to go.
REG: Oh…

> AARON *slings his backpack and heads for the door.* REG *looks up at his son, suddenly focused and clear.*

You're leaving, aren't you?
AARON: You never listen, Dad. I just said. I have to go.
REG: I know. But you're really leaving, aren't you?

> AARON *stops in his tracks, caught out. He nods.*

Good for you. I was gonna go away once. Got myself a motorbike and everything. Was gonna cross the Nullarbor, do the Top End, the works. One thing and another… it just never happened. Don't you make the same mistake.

> REG *looks small and lost.* AARON *can see some of his father's pain.*

AARON: Are you and Mum breaking up?

REG: I should've gone when I had the chance.

> *The two men face each other, both incapable of giving the other what he needs.*

I'm sorry. I love you. I wish I hadn't hit you, son.

AARON: Wishing doesn't do you any good, Dad. All you ever do is wish.

> AARON *goes to leave.* REG *stands, reaches into his pocket for his wallet.*

REG: You'll need some money.

AARON: I don't want anything from you.

> AARON *leaves.* REG *calls after him.*

REG: You're not the only one who's disappointed, Aaron. You're so wrapped up in your own bloody world. You're not the only who feels let down. You're not the only one.

> REG *watches his son go, then returns to the table and continues cleaning the gun.*

SCENE SEVENTEEN

Friday night.

Music and sounds of the deb ball leak out of the school gym into the night air.

DESLEY *is pacing.* RITA *comes out, looking for* AARON.

RITA: You sure you won't come inside, Des.

DESLEY: He's not coming.

RITA: His dad's late too. Perhaps the two of them are… [*She can't think what they'd be doing together.*] Perhaps they're just running late.

DESLEY: He's not coming. [*Beat.*] Aren't you worried about him?

> *Of course she is. Before* RITA *can respond,* BUSHY *comes out, sees what's happening. He offers* DESLEY *his arm, making the best of a bad situation.*

BUSHY: Looks like it's you and me, Desley.

> *She shakes her head.*

Save me a dance?

DESLEY: I will, Bushy.

He takes RITA*'s arm.*

BUSHY: [*in Shakespearean demeanour*] Sit, good cousin Capulet; for you and I are past our dancing days.

They go back into the gym, leaving DESLEY *to wait for* AARON.

Eventually AARON *arrives, dishevelled, wearing the dress suit, jacket and jeans. He has the soggy, smouldering remains of Bushy's cigar hanging out of his mouth.*

He's drunk.

AARON *sees* DESLEY *in her dress and gives a low whistle. She's not impressed. He walks around a bit, then offers her the cigar.*

AARON: Puff?

DESLEY: Where've you been?

AARON: Trouble with the tie.

DESLEY: You're not funny, Aaron.

AARON: What's up your arse, Des?

DESLEY: I've been here since six. You said you'd be here too.

AARON: Give me a break, will you? I'm sick.

DESLEY: Bullshit.

AARON: Bullshit? Look, proof.

He holds up the bottle of pills.

DESLEY: Why'd you even bother coming?

He moves in on her, trying to force her to dance.

AARON: You made me promise, remember? We were gonna have a little dance.

DESLEY: Get off.

AARON: Who's not in the mood to dance now? [*Shuffling in a mock dance*] Come on, Des. Isn't this why you came?

DESLEY *tears her shoes off and throws them at* AARON.

DESLEY: You want to dance? Here's some shoes.

She looks darkly at him.

AARON: I guess you changed your mind.

DESLEY: I guess I did.

AARON: Guess, guess, guess. [*He staggers up to the entrance to have a look in.*] Oooh… look at all the lights. Donny would've like this. We goin' in?

> DESLEY *doesn't answer. He ignores her. The colour and music and excited voices envelop him. He stands watching for a moment. His body becomes lighter and sways with the music. He shouts into the room.*

Bore it up her, Timsy!

> AARON *turns back to* DESLEY, *laughs, leers at her.*

Where'd you get the dress?

DESLEY: My dad got it for me.

AARON: You mean your foster dad. My dad's a real dad. Which means he does fuck-all. How do I look?

> *He twirls.*

DESLEY: You look nice.

AARON: You mean I look like shit. I fell down.

> *He opens his jacket to show her that his shirt is covered in mud.*

DESLEY: Okay. You look like shit. What's in the bag?

AARON: Wouldn't you like to know.

DESLEY: Not really.

AARON: You seen my mum? Where's my mum? You seen her yet?

DESLEY: Inside. Helping out.

AARON: That'd be right. Busy, busy, busy.

> *He looks at her dress again. He takes a closer look at the ruched bodice.*

I like your dress.

> DESLEY *doesn't want the compliment.*

[*Pointing at the ruching*] What d'you call that stuff?

DESLEY: It's called ruching.

AARON: Rooting?

> DESLEY *is embarrassed.*

DESLEY: Ruching.

AARON: Dress makes your tits stick out.

> *Now she's humiliated.*

You know, Donny always reckoned I should've put the hard word on you. He was always going on about it. How easy you'd be. What d'you reckon, Des?

DESLEY: Why are you being like this?

AARON: How about it? In memory of Donny?

He makes a clumsy lunge for her but she knees him in the balls.

DESLEY *composes herself. She could walk away right now, but she has something to say.* AARON *is still doubled over on the ground.*

DESLEY: I know what you're doing, Aaron.

AARON: Well at least someone does.

DESLEY: You're trying to make me hate you. You're trying to make everyone hate you so you can feel like all that pain isn't about Donny leaving you behind. Well you're not the only one who misses him, you know? You should stop this, Aaron. You don't want to lose any more friends. You don't want to make me hate you.

DESLEY *stops. She doesn't want to cry.* BUSHY *comes out, sees* DESLEY *run off.*

BUSHY: Desley?

BUSHY *looks at* AARON *getting back up on his feet.*

Give us your hand.

AARON: Leave me alone.

BUSHY: Let's just get you inside first.

AARON: I said fuck off, Bushy.

BUSHY: [*he's had enough*] Sure. Have it your own way, mate. I'll be inside if you need me.

AARON *picks up the cigar and brushes dirt of the end.*

AARON: I saved you some.

He finds this really funny. He starts laughing.

RITA *comes out and* AARON *finds this even funnier still, but pretty soon the laughter wears out. He realises what he's done, loses his bravado, lurches towards the gym and throws up.*

I've fucked up, haven't I?

BUSHY: There's worse things.

AARON: I'm sorry.

BUSHY: It was only ever a cigar, Aaron.

> BUSHY *tries to steer* RITA *back inside, but she's staying. He understands.* RITA *goes to her son.*

AARON: Where's Des?
RITA: She's gone.
AARON: I think I was a bastard to her.
RITA: She doesn't deserve that.
AARON: Shouldn't you be inside?

> RITA *shakes her head.*

Wouldn't want to keep you from something important.
RITA: Aaron.
AARON: Yeah. Okay.
RITA: It can't go on like this. None of us.
AARON: I'm going away for a while.

> RITA *stops herself from reacting.*

Aren't you gonna say something?
RITA: Going where? When?
AARON: Tonight. I called Sharon. She said I can stay with her, have her spare room. Might look for a job. Try and get some gigs.

> RITA *says nothing.*

I'll be alright.
RITA: I know.
AARON: You'll miss me.
RITA: I know.
AARON: I'll miss you too. Both of you. I will.
RITA: I know.
AARON: Is Dad alright?
RITA: I don't know.
AARON: I should go and find Des. See if she's okay.
RITA: When are coming back? Are you coming back?
AARON: [*with a shrug*] I'll keep in touch. It'll be better.
RITA: It'll be better.
AARON: You going back in?

> RITA *shakes her head.*

You going home?

> RITA *nods.*

Good.

> AARON *hugs his mum, an awkward, halfway hug.*
> *He finds his bag and leaves. She watches. He doesn't look back.*

SCENE EIGHTEEN

Friday night, late.
Now it's the bridge again.
The sound of a diesel train in the distance.

AARON *comes onto the bridge. He goes to the railing and looks over. He reaches into his backpack and finds the video cassette. He looks at it for a moment, then starts pulling the tape out of the cassette. When the tape has all spooled out onto the ground he hurls the whole lot over the edge and into the night.*

AARON: [*shouting at the night*] Take it back, you gutless prick. I don't want it anymore. I thought you knew what you wanted. I thought you had a plan. What happened to the plan, Donny? Wasn't it good enough? What happened to me? Wasn't I good enough?

> DESLEY *emerges from the shadows.* AARON *turns with a start when he hears her.*

He knew no-one cared about him, you know. He used to say it all the time. 'No-one gives a fuck about me.' He hated it here. He used to say, 'This bridge is fucked, doesn't go anywhere anymore'. But he liked the trains… 'All those people, they're going somewhere. Anywhere but here.' Donny reckoned one day the right train'd go under this bridge and take him away forever. Guess he was right about that.

> *They're both silent at the thought.*

DESLEY: It wasn't about you, Aaron. Just 'cos Donny fucked up, doesn't mean you have to.

AARON: I knew you'd be here.

DESLEY: [*with a shrug*] I think I know what's in the bag. [*He digs into his bag, pulls out her shoes and holds them up for her to see.*] Okay. Maybe I know what else is in the bag.

AARON: You gonna try and stop me?

DESLEY: [*shaking her head*] It's your life.
AARON: Doesn't feel like it.
DESLEY: You're not him, Aaron. If you leave, then leave because it's what you have to do.

    AARON *moves towards* DESLEY, *but she steps back from him.*

AARON: I don't want you to hate me, Des. I didn't mean what I said.
DESLEY: Which bit?
AARON: All of it. I'm sorry.

    She considers his apology.

DESLEY: You ever coming back?
AARON: [*with a shrug*] Would we still be friends if I did?
DESLEY: [*with a shrug*] Who knows?

    AARON *would like a farewell hug, but he thinks better of it.*

AARON: You could come with me, Des.

    She shakes her head.

Why not?
DESLEY: It's not what I want to do.

    They stand, facing each other for a moment.

    The sound of a diesel train in the distance.

AARON: Aren't you gonna say goodbye?
DESLEY: [*shaking her head*] It's bad luck.
AARON: What?
DESLEY: Saying goodbye to someone on a bridge. Means you'll never see them again.

    AARON *nods, picks up his bag, makes to leave.*

You can't go yet.

    AARON *turns. He doesn't know what she means.* DESLEY *puts her shoes on.*

You made me a promise.
AARON: What?
DESLEY: You promised you'd do my deb with me.
AARON: I said I was sorry.
DESLEY: I don't care. You're not going until you keep your promise.
AARON: I'll miss the train.

DESLEY: There's plenty of time.

> AARON *stands helplessly before his friend.*
>
> *The waltz begins to play.*

AARON: I don't know what to do.

> DESLEY *reaches out to him.*

DESLEY: Yes you do.

> *He takes her hand.* DESLEY *shows* AARON *how the deb was supposed to begin. He awkwardly follows her movements. She curtsies to him. He bows to her. She takes him by the hand and leads him into a dance.*
>
> DESLEY *and* AARON *dance together on the bridge.*
>
> *After a while,* AARON *steps away from* DESLEY, *picks up his backpack and walks away.*
>
> DESLEY *dances alone on the bridge.*
>
> *Lights and music slowly fade.*

THE END